NOT WHAT I SIGNED UP FOR

NOT WHAT
I SIGNED
UP FOR

Finding the Strength, Purpose, and Faith
to Get through a Season You Didn't Expect

Nicole Unice

TYNDALE
MOMENTUM®

A Tyndale nonfiction imprint

Visit Tyndale online at tyndale.com.

Visit Tyndale Momentum online at tyndalemomentum.com.

Visit the author at nicoleunice.com.

Tyndale, Tyndale's quill logo, *Tyndale Momentum*, and the Tyndale Momentum logo are registered trademarks of Tyndale House Ministries. Tyndale Momentum is a nonfiction imprint of Tyndale House Publishers, Carol Stream, Illinois.

Not What I Signed Up For: Finding the Strength, Purpose, and Faith to Get through a Season You Didn't Expect

Published in association with Jenni Burke of Illuminate Literary Agency: illuminateliterary.com.

The names and identifying details of some individuals whose stories appear in this book have been changed to protect their privacy.

For information about special discounts for bulk purchases, please contact Tyndale House Publishers at csresponse@tyndale.com, or call 1-855-277-9400.

Library of Congress Cataloging-in-Publication Data
A catalog record for this book is available from the Library of Congress.

ISBN 978-1-4964-4865-1

Printed in the United States of America

30 29 28 27 26 25 24
7 6 5 4 3 2 1

To Little Queen Mollie and her brave parents, JR and Stacie:
". . . this happened so that the works of God might be displayed . . ."

Contents

Foreword

I am a hard sell.

I don't want books to pitch me lofty, lovely ideas written from the pen of a perfect life—I want ones that talk to me like a human being. If authors don't consider that my situation might be complicated or my heartache might be raw, they don't have my attention.

Nicole Unice is an author who has my attention.

I met her some time ago at a local restaurant. After we'd been acquainted for years as fellow authors, she asked if I wanted to have dinner when she came to town. Over messy subpar nachos, the conversation went deep. For two hours, we barely came up for air. There was lots of head tilting (her) and fast talking (both of us), but I learned something important: Nicole was going to be a safe friend. I could tell because she was very, very honest.

Nicole was in the midst of a huge life transition with her family when we met for dinner that night. She didn't try to sugarcoat it. I have found, through the years, that when people who could be guarded choose instead to be vulnerable, you can trust them with your heart.

When I read *Not What I Signed Up For*, it felt like an extension of our dinner. Some books take a "time-share" approach to faith— they sell you on the possibilities of it, minimizing the less favorable realities so you'll buy in. Nicole doesn't do that. She gives voice to the difficult places while helping guide you to higher ground. She has the pastoral and counseling chops to write with authority . . . and yet, reading every page felt like having messy nachos with her while she shared her heart. Exactly the way I like my books and their authors: wise, warm, and a bit weathered.

Can I be completely honest? The last several years—from a pandemic to riots to political turmoil, from wars to natural disasters—have taken a huge toll on us. Many of us have turned into quite the skeptics and cynics. It reminds me a bit of a story my mother has told in our family for years.

The night my father was going to ask her to marry him, everything went wrong, leaving him feeling exasperated and defeated as they sat together in the car. Instead of sticking to his original romantic plan, he simply blurted out: *"Everything else is going wrong, I might as well ask you to marry me."* She said yes, so you could say that he still got the outcome he wanted. The beauty of this momentous moment, though, was laced with my father's skepticism and negativity.

Yes, it's been quite a couple of hard years. Sometimes I don't recognize the people we have become. Many of us have developed a *might as well* mentality. And we have paid a hefty price for our agreement to settle for that kind of half-hearted life.

Reading this book is an excellent step toward breaking that agreement. I know life hasn't been easy for you, but there is indeed more. It doesn't matter what your "not what you signed up for" issue is. What Nicole Unice wrote in these pages will help you.

Good news. You may be in the aftermath of a life you never asked for or wanted—or perhaps you're even still in the midst of one—but do not underestimate where God is in all of it.

With you. For you. Loving you to a better place.

Lisa Whittle
Author, Bible teacher,
host of *Jesus Over Everything* podcast

Losing the Horizon

I like to think of myself as an adventurous woman. I like to think that I not only accept but *embrace* change. I like to think that I can adapt, adjust, and go with the flow because I am a mature, responsible adult with a deep faith in a sovereign God. At least that's what I used to think.

One summer when Dave and I were still in the throes of parenting three young children, I decided to escape the monotony of the long, hot days by meeting my sister-in-law at our trailer by the lake, which was located on the border of North Carolina and Virginia. Two moms, six kids, and 350 square feet of trailer space—what could go wrong? Tracy and I coparented like champs, handling meals, activities, and conflict resolution with ease. On our second afternoon, we took the adventure up a notch and headed out on the pontoon boat for a little tubing. It started off great, but quickly sprang a leak—literally—when the tube semi-deflated and pulled the kids under as they were being towed behind a 100 hp motor.

Anyone who has owned a boat, attached a tube, or put kids on a tube behind a boat knows that the driver is always one brain cell away from completely losing their mind. Tracy, although quite helpful, had no experience driving a boat or directing the mechanics of tubing. As a result, I tried to drive the boat while reassuring the kids on the partially submerged tube that they would be *just fine*, but the crying from thirty yards behind the boat finally got to me. I jumped in like the lifeguard I imagine myself to be, Chaco sandals and all, and decided I would pull the tube in myself. Spoiler alert: I am not a lifeguard. I don't even like to swim with my face in the water.

Since I had only that one brain cell left, I failed to think through the ramifications of swimming to the tube without a life jacket—while the boat was adrift with no driver. Somehow in the chaos, I also managed to disconnect the tube rope from the boat. Despite my imaginative lifeguard status, I struggled to drag the tube back to the boat, which seemed to be rapidly floating away from us. I felt a little bubble of panic rise up in my chest. I was in the middle of a choppy lake, bobbing up and down while trying to keep my eyes on the three little kids on a deflating tube in the distance. At one point as I watched the boat drift farther and farther away, I saw Tracy smile and laugh with the other kids on the pontoon.

I had an out-of-body experience when I recognized that, unbeknownst to her, I was not okay. In fact, I was flailing and feeling like drowning was inevitable. I was stuck, not close enough to the tube to grab on and rest and not close enough to the boat to save us all. I was about to go under and take the three kids with me. But to her, the sun was still shining, the lake was still beautiful, and the boat was gently rocking on a warm summer day while I acted like I was totally in control and confident I could remedy this situation.

Somehow without revealing my near-death panic, I propelled myself and the kids back to the boat. After helping the kids scamper up the ladder, I heaved myself on board, started the motor, and guided us back to shore, never letting on how scared, helpless, and over my head I'd really been. What I knew without a doubt was that I never wanted to feel that way again, and I certainly didn't think it could get worse than that.

Spoiler alert: It can get worse.

Fast-forward several years. My world had upended. In the previous twenty-four months, everything had changed. I'd left a job I loved. My family had lost our church, community, and dear friendships; entered a global pandemic; sold our home. Now I was sitting in my car in a church parking lot, gathering the courage to walk into a church leadership gathering of several hundred people that I'd considered friends—even family. But by this point, I didn't know where I belonged. A foreign, gut-deep panic seemed to be my constant companion. I was gritting my teeth against the insecurity and fear that rose up in me, linked to the powerful, old lies that had been with me since before I could remember. As I sat in the parking lot, the insecurity was building a case against me, hurling accusations:

Yes, you do not belong. Yes, you've messed everything up.

This season caused me to question my work and every relationship I had—even the ones that appeared to be intact. I found myself adrift, not quite lost but certainly not found. I wondered whether it was even worth attempting to walk into this meeting without crying.

That afternoon in the parking lot was like hundreds of moments before it and hundreds more to come—moments when the pain of uncertainty was so palpable that it felt physical. *Who am I? Why is this happening?* And perhaps the hardest of all: *God, how could* this *be the plan?*

The panic I experienced in the in-between on the lake was nothing compared to the dread that ensued from these massive holes in my life. Losing so many things that I loved, that defined me, that shaped who I was and who I saw myself to be was so utterly unexpected that I couldn't find my bearings, couldn't touch solid ground.

A friend of mine described her own unexpected season like this: "Sometimes when learning to fly, pilots lose sight of the horizon because the sky and the ground look so similar. And when they lose the horizon, they don't even know if they are flying right side up." Losing the horizon is an honest metaphor of what we may experience during unexpected seasons.

In my work as a therapist, a pastor, and an author, I've had a front-row seat to more stories than most, and if there's one constant, it's this: Unforeseen events are always shocking to the person experiencing them, yet the reality is, these experiences are "normal." Even though we feel completely surprised in the moment, we know that most human beings will eventually experience the overwhelm of the unexpected. It comes to all of us, in one form or another, at some point.

I knew writing a book about uncertainty would be challenging—finding a way to leave space for the uniqueness of each person's story, finding a way to be helpful without being trite. When our souls have been singed with the fire of suffering, we are sensitive, prone to easily burn. I did not want to heap more guilt or shame into our already tender hearts. So I reached out to you, dear readers. I met you over Zoom in groups and individually, over email, and in person. We talked together from our homes, on my back patio, around soaring redwoods on an afternoon retreat. As we talked, you generously opened your hearts about your own unexpected seasons:

- Robert, who was downsized from his job and diagnosed with multiple sclerosis in the same week
- Nancy, who discovered her husband's affairs and then found herself divorced and unemployed after thirty-five years of marriage
- Mariella, who left the church she grew up in because of a painful conflict between her pastors (who were also her parents) and the church board
- Jonah, who after a decade of infertility, became the dad of twins with special needs, only to watch the stress and financial burden slowly erode his relationship with his wife and create a joyless marriage

- Callie, whose business partner and best friend of ten years sabotaged their business behind her back and ruined Callie's reputation

The circumstances are different, but the pattern is nearly always the same: Most unexpected seasons are precipitated by an unwelcome change and characterized by an unknown timeline and unsure outcome. Such events force our hand, pressing us to deal with our doubt and evaluate our faith and belief in a good God. They lead to questions of identity, struggles with grief, and a deep test of our ability to hope. There's no one way to describe this season, but you shared with me words that fall into two categories:

> Most unexpected seasons are precipitated by an unwelcome change and characterized by an unknown timeline and unsure outcome.

Disorientation: *maze, tumbleweed, desert*
Darkness: *black hole, dark cloud, deep fog*

Perhaps my favorite way to describe these seasons is "a pit" because that's where our journey will begin—following the story of a betrayed teenager, far from home, deep in a pit. It's a story from the Bible with enough twists and turns to keep us guessing—and so many opportunities to learn more about ourselves, about God, and about His presence and care in even the worst of situations. If you know what it feels like to carry panic because your own life story has become so dark or so disorienting, if you feel like you've lost the horizon, you will identify with the story of Joseph. His story spans a significant portion of the book of Genesis, which covers several decades of Joseph's life, from his teenage years to fatherhood, from the pit to the palace to the prison and back again. We'll take a slow walk together through his story, investigating and discovering together how God showed up in Joseph's life—and how He shows up in ours.

Maybe you wonder how helpful a guide Joseph will really be as you navigate your own disappointment. I can think of two reasons for this: First, you may think you already know everything there is to know about Joseph. After all, he's one of the few biblical characters to show up as the leading character in a Broadway musical![1]

A second reason you might doubt that you can relate to Joseph's experience is simply that you know the shiny ending. It's easy to read a Bible story with the end in mind. If you know how Joseph's story turns out, you may not fully engage with his experience. You may also doubt God would ever work in the same dramatic way in your own life. I know that as I've wrestled through Joseph's story over the years, I've heard a niggling voice in the back of my mind: *Sure must have been nice for Joseph to have things turn out so well.* I lacked faith to believe that God could do as much redeeming and reconciling work in my story. I chose a settled resentment and detached apathy rather than a hopeful acceptance of what God is doing and will continue to do in my own life.

But by lingering in the in-between part of Joseph's story—thirteen years of captivity and imprisonment with no end in sight—you'll learn how to persevere when you have no idea how your own story will end. As you witness his eventual restoration and redemption unfolding in an entirely different way from what he must have expected, you'll find hope that God will orchestrate the events in your life too.

In fact, within Joseph's story you will find signposts for your journey through the seasons you didn't sign up for—tests of character, trust developed through trials of faith, and triumphs of forgiveness, redemption, and hope. You'll discover what it means to believe that God has good intentions for you and that you can rest in His faithfulness and plan. As you do, you'll discover a resilient faith on the other side of your season.

If you've picked up this book because you are in one of those unexpected seasons, I pray that you'll feel seen and understood here. I can promise you that I won't placate or patronize you with pithy answers or viral quotes. I'm not here to heap more pain into a season you are trying to understand or reconcile, but I am here to invite you to experience your story through the biblical stories God has invited us to enter—stories that teach us about ourselves, about our humanity, and about God's presence with us from beginning to end. But unlike sitcoms, fairy tales, and every other "get there fast" narrative in our culture, this story embraces all our humanity—the good, the bad, the broken, the unexpected.

In each chapter we'll focus on Joseph's ordeal and the stories of people today who are somewhere in the process of being tested, whose trust has been challenged and stretched, and who are triumphing in spite of their circumstances. My hope is that the prayers I've written and the stories you read will encourage you to persevere. And if you have made it through an unexpected season, I pray this book will encourage you to look back and discern even more deeply that God has been present with you in every valley, in every pit; that when you lost the horizon, God did not; and that even in your loneliest moment, you were never alone.

In order to journey fully alongside Joseph, you might also check out the related study guide and video series, which dive even more deeply into the story of Joseph and his family, tracing the incredible thread of redemptive love that God reveals to us from Genesis to Revelation. Through exercises, prompts, and discoveries in God's Word, this guide will enable you to enter into your own story with eyes to see God's redemption for you. You can use the guide individually or with a group. Groups can feel awkward or uncomfortable at first, but reflecting and interpreting our stories alongside of God's Word—*His* stories—is incredibly powerful. It's the power of our individual testimonies that continues to witness to who God is—even (and especially) in our unexpected seasons.

During a discovery session I held with some of you, dear readers, our conversation turned to the lessons learned along the way, and one of you said, "In the midst of my unexpected season, I'm at peace anyway." The others there murmured in agreement, perhaps sending up their own quick prayer. And that might be the best prayer we can claim, no matter where we are on the journey:

God, give me peace anyway.

CHAPTER 1

BELIEVE THE DREAM

The greatest need of collective humanity . . .
is renovation of our hearts.

DALLAS WILLARD, *Renovation of the Heart*

What do I do when I don't know what to do?

This is my prayer in loss, my most honest prayer, one I've prayed countless times over the past several years. Sometimes in the worst moments of my own unexpected season, I would wait for nightfall when I could go outside and lie on my back in the darkest place I could find—the patio, the grass, the driveway . . . even the cul-de-sac outside our house. When I was at my most disoriented, my spiritual practice was simply to lie down and look up. Seeing stars, repositioning myself as a small, tiny being in the vast space of the galaxy was the only way to find my bearings for one more day.

On a particularly bad day in the middle of this time, I was doing what I do best—venting my anxiety and frustration on the nearest living thing. My husband, Dave, and I were fighting. I was bringing every burden and resentment to a head, lashing out at him as if our petty disagreement was my actual problem; as if solving that one issue or winning this one argument would some-how fix every other wound I was trying to heal, every other wrong I was trying to vindicate. It was a *very* cold December day, and when I walked out of the house that night and was lying on the driveway, I couldn't find peace with the stars. The ambient light of our Christmas decorations felt like noise, matching the ongoing clamor in my own heart. All the hurt, anger, grief, and unknowns inside squeezed me like a vise. This anxious pressure demanded movement, so I walked down our dark street and then along a little path to the nearby golf course. I needed to seek out that very darkest spot on earth so I could see the brightest lights in heaven. I lay on the grass and shivered, holding my own self tight, breathing into the night air and hearing the cry of my soul:

This is not what I signed up for.

"Not what I signed up for" carried the proper weight for the middle of that season. My unmet expectations were mixed with a deeper sense of confusion and grief—anger, unforgiveness, dis-appointment, and fear, all crumpled into a tight ball that took up its dwelling in the center of my chest. The kicker is that this mass of emotion and pain wasn't the worst problem—the unknown timeline was. How long would it be this way? How would I survive? And who would I be on the other side of this season—if there even was an "other side"? The one moment of panic was painful; the unknown length and outcome felt excruciating.

Perhaps "not what I signed up for" is our modern-day lament, words given to shape our true, living-on-this-earth experience.

Our Human Response

When faced with a season we didn't expect and don't want, we may try to deal with the pain in one of two ways. On one end of the "not what I signed up for" spectrum are the "skip and stuff" people. Skipping and stuffing is an attempt to minimize our pain by jumping to a future happy ending as a way to pretend all is well. However, painful emotions won't pretend, and they can't be skipped over. They keep coming, and they require a response. Avoiding, ignoring, or denying the pain is a short-term solution that creates long-term damage. Our bodies hold our pain and memories of unhealed storylines, so when we encounter a similar situation, we don't operate out of a place of health or presence. Instead, whether we acknowledge it or not, we respond out of the pain of our past. Skipping and stuffing tends to lead to superficial living. The number of situations we have to avoid, reframe, or ignore grows over time, and what once felt like a positive way to cope becomes destructive to our relationships, our purpose, and our very soul.

On the other end of the spectrum is the temptation to "dive and dwell." Unlike the skip and stuffers, people on this end of the spectrum dive right into the deep end of pain. They are willing to say what's gone wrong, who's hurt them, and what they are struggling with, but they can get stuck inside the dive and end up dwelling in the pain. Eventually, diving and dwelling ends up feeling like drowning, and these people tend to overidentify with the pain in their stories. They lose hope, live out their victimization story, and arc toward despair.

You may immediately identify with one side of the spectrum or the other, or you may realize that you can swing back and forth depending on the situation. But here's the promise: God offers us another way.

What unexpected seasons offer is a different way of viewing life: God's hand, God's plan, and our faith to withstand. He invites you to the narrow middle of the spectrum, where you can "release and reengage." The narrow middle requires surrender—releasing what you expected and then reengaging your life from a new perspective. To do so takes compassion and courage—for yourself and for your future. But the results are beautiful because this narrow middle is where redemption is promised. Right here in the middle is where you can acknowledge and make space for what's painful, what's lost, what's unjust. But the middle is also where you can, as Scripture says, grieve with hope, dream with confidence, and live with joy.[1] That hope is found in connection to a much greater story and in the faith and willingness to relentlessly pursue the renewed storyline in your own life. As you do this, you will become real and redeemed in the process.

Real and redeemed people are re-created people, made in the image of God and moving toward the holiness of Christ. Real and redeemed people are able to be fully present and at home in their stories, willing to embrace their own failures and ongoing patterns of brokenness. Real and redeemed people can look back at the storyline of their own lives and acknowledge that there is real pain and struggle, but they also believe, as we'll see with Joseph, that even that which was intentionally planned to harm them, to silence them, to minimize them can be used for good in God's hands. Real and redeemed people see that blessing appears when they are pliable in God's hands and open to His story, giving Him all of it—the questions, the unknowns, the undone, the unforgiven—and letting

> Within God's story we discover purpose for our pain, faith in our uncertainty, and compassion in our grief.

Him guide them into the most real version of themselves. Within God's story we discover purpose for our pain, faith in our uncertainty, and compassion in our grief. Only a broken heart has the capacity to expand, and choosing the real and redeemed path is the way to that expanded heart—for God, for yourself, and for the world.

The promise of redemption is true, but first we must respond to the difficulties themselves, whether we are navigating present challenges or are looking back at a rocky season, trying to make sense of it all. The cry of the broken heart is not just the pain of the wound or loss; it's the agony of the unknown timeline and unsure outcome. In Psalm 74, God's people lament,

> *We are given no signs from God;*
>   *no prophets are left,*
>   *and none of us knows how long this will be.*

PSALM 74:9

So maybe the honest statement "not what I signed up for" puts us squarely in the middle of the experience of God's people throughout the ages—this dark, disturbing time when what we believed to be God's plan is obliterated, our hearts are shattered, and there's no timeline or end in sight.

God, what do we do when we don't know what to do?

When we feel, as the psalmist describes, that we have no signs from God, no prophet or encourager to spur us forward, when words fail and life leaves a bitter taste in our mouths, when we feel utterly abandoned and lost, we still have one powerful, transforming thing:

We still have God's stories.

The stories God tells are designed to invite us in, to help us translate and interpret our own experience of faith through those who have gone before us. God's stories are markers along a twisting path. When we find ourselves lost, we can look for these wayfinders in the wilderness: the courageous men and women who've prayed for bread, who've confronted kings, or who've endured famines, fights, and fatigue to seek God, to stay faithful, and to take one more step forward. Eugene Peterson says it this way: "When we submit our lives to what we read in Scripture, we find that we are not being led to see God in our stories but our stories in God's. God is the larger context and plot in which our stories find themselves."[2]

It takes faith to look up from your circumstances and your pain and believe that God invites you into a life of biblical proportions, a life in which *God* is the larger context. *He* is the larger plot. The people you read about in the Bible are surrounded by circumstances that feel far different from your disappearing online retirement account or the hospital machine whirring next to your loved one or the tedium of another day in a job you dread—but somehow these humans in the Bible are surprisingly still a lot like you and me. They are humans caught up in the circumstances of their world and their pain, who have choices to make when unexpected seasons blow into their lives. It's easy to gloss over these stories as ancient fables or the stuff of children's Sunday school lessons. It actually takes courage and grit to believe that you can get to know these characters in Scripture and that you—yes, you yourself—are *a character in God's narrative*.

As I acknowledged in the introduction, I realize you might wonder why I've chosen to focus on Joseph—in fact, you might think that's actually a bad or irrelevant idea. I mean, isn't Joseph the guy who had spectacular dreams about his leadership and influence and then lived through a Disney-movie-like adventure? In the end, didn't he get everything he envisioned? Didn't God restore his whole family in the process? These are the same kinds of questions I've confronted in myself:

> "Isn't it a little far-fetched to identify with a tribal family from the ancient Near East thousands of years ago?"
> "Do you actually think this dumpster fire of a life I'm living right now can actually be fully restored, like Joseph's story?"
> "Are you saying I can keep believing the dreams I have in my life, even when all seems lost?"

I've come to believe that this story is an invitation from God Himself:

- Come and see.
- Come and see what's actually hidden in the details of this story.

- Come and see how I move in unexpected ways.
- Come and see how Joseph lives in the tension of his own sorrow and his faith.
- Come and see how tests and trials do eventually lead to triumph, but not in a way that anyone could anticipate.
- Come and see how Joseph's story is your story.
- Come and see My faithfulness in your "not what I signed up for" season.

As we walk through the details of Joseph's story, we are going to discover that our stories, like his, are full of wayfinding markers. Our trials will most certainly look different, but many of our questions will be the same:

- What does it look like to walk forward when every choice feels impossible?
- How do I prosper in even the most difficult moments, and what does prospering mean anyway?
- How do I keep living with hope when all signs point to the death of my dream?
- What do I do with my grief, sorrow, and pain?
- How do I forgive?
- What does true restoration mean on earth? What can I really hope for, and how do I keep hoping?
- What does redemption look like in my life, and how do I recognize it?
- Can I really trust God?

Start with the Ending

As you think about your story, you will likely find that you have some of these same questions (and more). So before we get into the details, I want to take you to the ending of Joseph's story. When our lives become unpredictable, we crave predictability.

This is the reason for the enormous uptick in viewing old sitcoms during the COVID-19 pandemic[3]—with so much stress swirling through our lives, our brains craved the comfort and certainty of a twenty-two minute show with a structured format and predictable ending. Ironically, this is one of the many reasons I've come to see the Bible as God's true and inspired Word: If humans wrote the Bible out of their own intellect, we would tie everything up in a bow, delineate clear heroes and villains, and end up with a book of stories that read like spun myths, cheesy sitcoms, and superhero movies.

In sitcoms and movies, we look for circumstances and characters that are framed for us in ways that create the predictable loops and comfort we desire. Even if that movie is a murder mystery or that novel is a devastatingly sad love story, it still follows a format that can help our brains relax into predictability. We escape into a world where conflict comes to a head, murders are solved, and love wins.

Since I know your season feels so out of control, maybe spoiling the ending is just what you need. Here's the flyover version of the whole Joseph story in case you haven't read it in a while. (By the way, now would be a great time to pause and read the whole story: You can find it in Genesis 37–50.)

As a boy, Joseph grew up in the glow of being "the favorite"—the favorite son of Jacob, his father, because his mother, Rachel, had been the love of his father's life. This status came with favor that exceeded that of his ten older brothers (all from other mothers), who grew jealous and resentful of him. Like many popular children, Joseph was either unaware or unfazed by his brothers' animosity, going so far as to share a dream with them that implied that one day his brothers would bow to him. They did not receive this well, and when given the chance, the older brothers schemed to kill him—though they ended up faking his death and selling him to some traders instead. The favored son then became a slave and was taken out of his own land to Egypt, becoming a house slave to one of Pharaoh's officials before being falsely accused of a crime and unjustly imprisoned. Years went by, but after an incredible chance to interpret a dream of Pharaoh's, Joseph was suddenly elevated to second in command in all of Egypt, preparing the country for famine that was predicted in Pharaoh's dream. When the famine came to pass, Joseph's brothers traveled to Egypt for food. Joseph's teenage dream was realized: They bowed before their brother, whom they did not recognize. Joseph revealed himself to them, forgave them for their treachery, and was even restored to his beloved father—saving his family in the process. The End.

It's definitely worth a full read—as this rapid flyover doesn't do the story justice. But on first glance, it's easy to see how Cinderella-like the story appears. Joseph, young and handsome, making his way through a foreign land and coming out triumphant. It seems that way—except for a few details in these chapters of Genesis. Like the fact that Joseph was betrayed and abandoned by his own brothers, who then covered up their lies for decades. And an unsavory and quite explicit story about Judah, Joseph's older brother, which gives us a taste of what life was really like in those days. And that little detail about thirteen years passing between when Joseph was sold and when he was reunited with his family. And all the tears shed along the way that reveal his deep grief and sorrow. Maybe it wasn't such a rags-to-riches story after all.

In fact, I'm sure Joseph could relate to the reader who described her own season as "drowning in a sea of unexpectedness." During all of his twenties and much of his thirties, Joseph's life went from bad to worse—from slave to prisoner—with every hope dashed and good deed forgotten. I don't know whether Joseph, like me, dreamed of stars in the sky, trying to remind himself that he was part of a much bigger story than he could see in the darkness.

We do know this: Joseph didn't forget his dreams—or the God who gave them to him. In fact, as we'll see, by the time he was reunited with his brothers, Joseph's greatest treasure wasn't found in his exalted social status and wealth but in the settled peace and security he'd found in God.

The best part? God wants to give those same treasures to you and me today. To find this treasure is to turn away from the temptation to skip and stuff or to dive and dwell. It's to release your expectations and face a new reality. It's to take one small, faltering step after another into God's way.

On a warm fall day, I found myself, once again, in an unexpected moment. I had pulled over at a little country park, waiting for the virtual appointment with my spiritual director to begin. My life was still off-kilter and in transition, so it seemed fitting that I sat there eating a Dairy Queen Blizzard while evaluating the state of my soul. I was reminded of other moments over the past few years when I'd sat in my car in a parking lot, wishing I were in bed under the covers. Instead, I was headed to another event where I would need to arrange my face and soul to face questions I couldn't answer: *Why did you leave? What are you doing now? What really happened?*

Years later, the questions remained. But the near-constant panic that I felt at the beginning of this "not what I signed up for" season had mellowed; in its place, I often discovered moments of nostalgia, pensive wisdom, a bit of settled sadness.

I put in my earbuds and walked down a footpath before sitting on a log and signing in to my virtual appointment. I prepared to answer the question Susan always asked: "How's your life with God?" As usual, I thought to myself: *I have no idea how my life with God is.* I was getting comfortable with not knowing, though, because I'd learned that God shows up anyway. I didn't have to pretend or posture with Him.

I looked out from my perch to a path framed with trees in autumnal glory, vibrant shades of red, gold, green. It was beautiful. The metaphor wasn't lost on me—the beauty of the leaves also signified the change ahead. In just a few short weeks the trees would be bare, the path dark. The cycle of growth followed by change and loss would continue, headed into the barrenness of winter. The hope of renewal is only believed by faith when the season goes dark. I didn't know that winters in the soul could also be so dark and so long. I found myself wondering how much of my unexpected season had been about leaving the path I wanted to be on—releasing my expectations and my vision for what life needed to look like, of how I expected (demanded?) God to show up.

I stared through the trees and down the gravel path that stretched ahead of me, ambling upward and around, disappearing out of sight. I couldn't tell where the path was going—but it was beautiful, and it was going somewhere. I finished my call, and I decided to enter the metaphor, walking a few paces down the path. I looked up between the kaleidoscope of colors dancing in the breeze, and I found myself saying yes to God again, surrendering to His way again, choosing Him again. This is the path of the unexpected season: We don't know where it's going, but we can trust that God is with us, that God is for us, and that eventually—the season will change.

To get there takes a choice: *Will you release the path you expected and choose to follow Him instead?*

A PRAYER OF RELUCTANT YES

Lord,

I'm confused about this path,
which seems to be taking me further away from
what seems good,
and what feels safe,
and what is known.
But seeing as all the other paths have disappeared
and I don't want to stay here alone,
I guess I'll go with You.
Will You be patient with me as I learn how to trust
that You know the way?

Amen.

CHAPTER 2

HOLD ON TO THE PROMISES

*When you're in the intersection between the promises of
God and the details of your situation, what you do with
your mind is very important. In this intersection, God will
never ask you to deny reality. . . . Faith doesn't deny reality.
No, it is a God-focused way of considering reality.*

PAUL DAVID TRIPP, *Dangerous Calling*

In the summer of 2019, I started my "things I don't know" list.
The list was long, painful, and extensive. It covered my vocation,
my relationships, my marriage, my inner world. The entries blos-
somed as we entered the pandemic in March 2020. Here are a few
selections, straight from my tearstained journal:

- September 20, 2019: I don't know who's for me, who's
  against me, or who's indifferent to me.
- April 5, 2020: I don't know if my faith is growing.
- April 15, 2020: I don't know if anyone I love will get sick
  or die from coronavirus.
- May 2020: I don't know if I'll ever preach again.
- November 2020: I don't know who my friends are.
- January 2021: I don't know where God's sending me.

But I kept a "what I do know" list as well. One entry was short, a prayer to the God I knew even when I couldn't feel or see or perceive Him near me:

- I know You are intentional.
- I know You are purposeful.
- I know You are kind.

Writing out my prayers and lists—and many times, simply finding a Bible verse to copy into my journal—was a coping mechanism, a survival tactic to acknowledge God and His goodness. These brief reflections were often the only thing my heart could grab on to when it felt as if the world had fallen out from under me.

Here's the truth about unexpected seasons: They are always an invitation to build a deeper and more resilient faith. And that faith is based on one certainty: Our circumstances aren't predictable, but God's character always is.

You and I don't have to doubt or second-guess who God is because He is love. He is truth. Even in the darkest, most confusing times, the truth of God still stands. He is still love. He is still at work. He is still near. In the upcoming chapters, you'll discover that your hardships can actually move you closer to Him in a way that yields life, but this season will require much from you:

What may change is your understanding and definition of love and truth.

What may grow is a deeper sense of your own relentless craving to be in control.

What may be awakened is a recognition of the comfort and security you expect from your circumstances.

What may have to be plowed up is your sense of safety that is tied to predictability.

What may be toppled are the idols that have taken up residence in your soul. These appetites and assumptions pretend to be God, act like God, and sound like God but are actually just self-shaped beliefs that are not strong enough to withstand the hurricane of trouble, grief, sorrow, or uncertainty that accompanies unwelcome events.

When we turn our attention to Joseph, we have little evidence of exactly how he processed the thirteen years he spent in captivity and slavery. But by the end of the story, we see evidence of a maturity of character and trust in God that were forged in the darkness. Here's how we know: After going through the very worst of an unexpected season, a time full of tests and trials, a season in which Joseph had every reason to fear, every reason to become bitter or vindictive, every reason to believe that he had been betrayed—not just by his family but by God—he speaks words of truth and hope. These are the words of Joseph to his brothers, and they give us a window into how Joseph interpreted his own story. I believe they apply to our own seasons today:

> By the end of Joseph's story, we see evidence of a maturity of character and trust in God that were forged in the darkness.

Don't be afraid. Am I in the place of God? You intended to harm me, but God intended it for good to accomplish what is now being done, the saving of many lives.
GENESIS 50:19-20

After Joseph reconnects with his brothers and father, after the suffering and sorrow refine and smooth his character, after he matures and accepts the calling God places on his life, he looks back at all that has happened over more than a decade and reassures his brothers—the very ones who betrayed him and left him for dead. And those three sentences give us the framework of hope we all desperately need in our own times of darkness. Joseph's words reveal the promises you can rely on, can stake your life upon. These are a flicker of light—pulled straight from Joseph's declaration—in what might be the very darkest night of your soul.

1. Do not be afraid.
2. God is here.
3. God has plans to accomplish good for you and through you.

These are the promises of a predictable God no matter how unpredictable the circumstances.

1. Do Not Be Afraid

Fear does a number on us. It causes us to shrink in and step back. Fear turns us inward—focusing our energy on protecting ourselves. Fear builds walls, pacifying us with self-created protection that is neither real nor helpful. The problem with walls is that, though they might keep bad things out, they also keep the good things from coming in. Those walls are like a house of cards printed with a stone facade, a mirage of protection that can topple with the slightest breeze. Fear will keep us paralyzed, neither able to move forward nor grow through our pain. That's why acknowledging our fear is one of the most important steps we can take in our uncertainty.

Fear can be overcome in one of three ways: We connect with someone who helps us move through a fear, we gain strength by surviving the fear that comes to us, or we find the courage to face the fear with a new frame of mind. And God provides all three within Himself.

The first thing God provides is His indwelt presence. Fear triumphs when it gets us to feel alone. We can be surrounded by people yet still believe no one *quite* gets it; no one is present enough, caring enough, or wise enough to actually face the fear with us. And part of that is absolutely true. No one can experience your exact feelings, understand your thoughts, and hold your story—past and present—together in a way that brings full understanding. This is why it's such a great compliment when someone tells you they feel seen by you. But "feeling seen" usually lasts for a moment. Only a spiritual presence can fully understand another's whole self—body, mind, and soul. This is why Jesus told His disciples that it would be better for them when He left and they received the Holy Spirit. The Holy Spirit, Jesus told them, is the One who "dwells with you" (John 14:17, ESV; see also 2 Timothy 1:14). The power and presence of the Spirit gives us both the comfort and courage to move through fear.

The second thing God gives is the ability to persevere by changing our perspective on life-and-death circumstances. Although we still may feel the crushing weight of loss and grief, although we may feel we can hardly bear to continue forward, God calls this—yes, the very season you are in—"light and momentary troubles" (2 Corinthians 4:17) compared to the eternal glory reserved for his children. We must understand that God is not calling our troubles "light," as if we are supposed to just pull ourselves up and get on with it. But *in comparison* to what's to come, the troubles become light.

We've had the opportunity to take our kids on several family trips. Our daughter used to dread flights of any length—until we flew to South Africa and spent twenty hours flying. Short flights used to be unbearable, but *in comparison* to spending a day and a night in one airplane seat, the shorter flights became "light and momentary troubles." Yes, it takes great faith to shift our mindset—but every single hardship in your darkest hour, compared to the glorious reality of what's to come, will seem light. Can we believe this on our own strength? *Absolutely not.* But is it true? *Absolutely.*

The third thing that God supplies is a frame of mind that allows us to face the fear directly. Sometimes we gain a new frame of mind because it's the only option. We are so helpless, so uncertain that we really have no other choice. Why do people always pray in hospital waiting rooms? Because that is the only option when the fate of their loved one is out of their hands and they have to wait and trust. What do we do when we face a season of life that feels like it's pulling us so hard it will tear us apart? At some point, the only place we can ground ourselves is on our knees, seeking the mercy of God who can give us just enough courage to face one more day.

Yes, *do not be afraid* is the first thing we need to hear in our unexpected seasons. We cannot count on a world that won't make us fearful, but we can count on a God who abundantly provides the only way to move beyond fear.

2. God Is Here

Time and time again, Joseph gave the credit and the glory where it belonged. Ultimately he declared, "Am I in the place of God?" (Genesis 50:19). It might seem easy for Joseph to say this—especially at the end of the story when the dream came true and reconciliation happened. But Joseph believed this *before* he knew the end of the story, as we will see. Even in the midst of suffering, Joseph lived in acceptance of God's plans because he understood his own place in the universe.

To acknowledge that "God is here" is to know that God is both present with us *and* in control of our situation. Joseph understood that God is altogether unlike us—that He is holy, sovereign, and majestic over all—the happy and the hard, the best and the worst. The God of the universe cannot be manipulated or appeased for personal gain.

When Scripture uses the term "the fear of the Lord," it is describing this sovereign aspect of God. Ironically, a proper fear of the Lord allows us to overcome our own fears by "worshiping Him and regarding Him as truly awesome."[1] To do so is to believe that He is fully aware and fully in control, no matter what—and it is to worship Him even in our affliction.

In the time of Joseph, what set God apart as the Lord of the Israelites was the fact that He was one God, supreme over all. When Joseph was brought to Egypt, he was surrounded by people worshiping many gods. Even the king of Egypt, Pharaoh, was considered a god in human form. In a culture of many idols and gods whom people had to appease with offerings to get what they wanted—fertility, wealth, power, knowledge—Joseph knew there was only one God. Though we may not see people worshiping visible idols today, we are surrounded by people worshiping and appeasing invisible idols—comfort, safety, prosperity, human approval.

Like Joseph, we all will be tested by our uncertainty: *Is God still in control when everything feels out of control?* What we see in Joseph is a gritty belief to know that *God is here*—that God was "here" even when he was in the pit, even when he was in a foreign land, even in the worst of his circumstances. We also see that Joseph had humility—a right understanding of his place in the universe and God's power as sovereign. He reminds us that our character isn't shaped so much in moments of fair weather and blue skies—it's simply revealed for what was already there when the storm hit. And Joseph's dogged understanding of both humility and sovereignty is a rock-solid foundation, even in the most poignant parts of his season of suffering.

3. God Has Plans to Accomplish Good for You and through You

The full nature of God can only be revealed with this third promise. We need the first two promises in order to believe the third. God gives us Himself; His presence that is both with us and in control allows us to move past fear and into trust. Then God, in time, reveals His purposes: *God has plans*. This third promise enables us not just to survive our unexpected seasons but to see them as the rich soil for future growth, a place of deep roots and abundant flourishing. It's in Joseph's final comforting words to his brothers that we embrace the fullness of his knowledge of God and his own story's narrative. As Joseph looks back at all that has happened over more than a decade, he is able to say with conviction:

God intends. Let that sink in for a minute. God had a reason for Joseph's captivity and incarceration. God has purposes. God has thoughts and motivations toward you. God has an interest in you and your life. God is involved with you.

God has plans. His inclination toward you is not like that of a benevolent but disinterested father who attends his child's basketball game because he has nothing more pressing or interesting to do. This is not a father who stands on the sidelines but one who gets involved. God's plans are about inclination with action. God has plans for you. Even when things feel out of hand, they are never out of His hands.

God has plans to accomplish good. The two Hebrew words used most commonly for the work of "accomplishing" or "making something" are *bara* and *asah*. The term *bara* always has God as its subject and is generally used for a new creation—making something out of nothing. For example, this is the word used to describe God's activity in Genesis 1:1. Meanwhile, when the word *asah* refers to "making something," it usually describes making something out of what already is—refashioning what's already there. So the word *asah* often captures the idea of re-creating, refinishing, redeeming what already is into something different, something more—something good.

When Joseph talks about God's plans in his story, the word used is not *bara*—this isn't about God wiping every bad thing from Joseph's memory and starting fresh. Instead, it's the word *asah*: "You intended to harm me, but God intended it for good to accomplish [*asah*] what is now being done" (Genesis 50:20). In that little word we hear the deep truth that the days, months, and years when Joseph was separated from his father, betrayed by his brothers, sold into slavery, and thrown into prison while holding on to a dream that seemed as far-fetched as being summoned by Pharaoh himself—none of it was wasted. All of it had *asah* energy behind it because of a God who does not just hold the power of creation in His hand—He holds the power of re-creation. He refashions evil purposes and the plans of flawed, forgetful, or even hostile people and uses them for His good. And His good is not just *for* you—He has good He intends to occur *through* you. This is not just about God vindicating you or your cause, although that sometimes happens. This is about something much, much greater. In all of the pain and struggle, in the tears and the waiting, in the holding out hope for a dream that never seems to be coming, God is not just about you, He's about what's happening through you.

Joseph did not see his story as one in which he was the righteous hero whom God rescued just for the sake of shaming his brothers. No! Joseph saw that every good God intended was related to other good plans—for other people. In fact, I would argue that Joseph's suffering may have been intentionally prolonged by God for a greater purpose, that all of Joseph's suffering was for a greater purpose that could not be realized one day sooner than it happened. Joseph himself tells the story that way—that every single twist and turn, even the darkest moments, had a good purpose that God could use. He knew that God's *asah* work in his circumstances was for an even greater purpose than his life alone.

In the sharpest points of your grief, in the exhausting wrestling of your sorrow and your unanswered questions, it may feel too hard to trust in a good God with a great plan. It may feel like you can't possibly step out in faith when you feel afraid.

But what if you did?

A PRAYER FOR WHEN WE DON'T KNOW HOW TO PRAY

God,

Help me believe that even now—
You are good.
That even still—
You are working.
That even when I see nothing but trouble ahead—
You see further still,
refashioning, re-creating, and redeeming all things.
Give me a steadfast heart for today
and eyes to see the long view with You.

Amen.

PART 1

TESTING

Testing: an investigation to determine the essential character of a person, especially integrity.

Hebrew-Greek Key Word Study Bible

Now Israel [Jacob] loved Joseph more than any of his other sons, because he had been born to him in his old age; and he made an ornate robe for him. When his brothers saw that their father loved him more than any of them, they hated him and could not speak a kind word to him.

Joseph had a dream, and when he told it to his brothers, they hated him all the more. . . .

So when Joseph came to his brothers, they stripped him of his robe—the ornate robe he was wearing—and they took him and threw him into the cistern. The cistern was empty; there was no water in it. . . .

When the Midianite merchants came by, his brothers pulled Joseph up out of the cistern and sold him for twenty shekels of silver to the Ishmaelites, who took him to Egypt.

GENESIS 37:3-5, 23-24, 28

CHAPTER 3

THE TEST OF LOSS

No literature is more realistic and honest in
facing the harsh facts of life than the Bible.

EUGENE H. PETERSON, *A LONG OBEDIENCE IN THE SAME DIRECTION*

I was loading leftover snacks into the back of her minivan when Whitney turned to me. Her daughter attended the high school Bible study I hosted in my home, and Whitney had volunteered to bring refreshments that day.

"I know you are a pastor . . . ," she said.

I winced a bit, struggling myself to make sense of my vocation just a few months into my own unexpected season.

Whitney continued, "My daughter's been diagnosed with cancer." Once again, I was caught off guard. This was a mom I barely knew, and she was telling me about an incredible and unexpected pain—and the loss that came with it. We stood behind her car in the early morning light while she shared her struggles—an unexpected diagnosis, an unsure outcome, all the anxiety that came with it. My heart ached for her, and I offered her what I had:

presence, a hug, some words of encouragement. Anyone driving by would see two moms clasping hands and seeking God's healing and strength. Because when your teenager has cancer, what else can you do?

In a sermon about Jesus washing His disciples' feet, pastor Tim Keller notes that in the Bible, we don't just get propositions or simple statements; we get stories, and stories are living pictures.[1] A picture brings richness and meaning to a principle. A picture is painted through story. You and I are each living a story right now, as are the people around us. Stories are the way we experience life—the way we make meaning out of what might otherwise seem random, inconsequential, or cruel. The curveballs of life seem to require a special kind of engagement, some way of making sense of things that aren't easy to understand. It's easy to understand a good and faithful God when things are going well. The equation seems to be *God is good = I have good things.* But when our world falls apart and God is still supposed to be good, we can't help but wrestle with what it all means. Circumstances like Whitney's are times of testing: places where what we have known and believed is challenged, where our own stories require us to reckon with what God's goodness looks like when it doesn't immediately—or ever—mean good things as we've defined them.

I'm so grateful that God has given us both principles and pictures in the Bible. And in particular, I'm thankful that God has given us the story of Joseph, which invites us to understand how the testing not just of our faith but of our character, motivations, and assumptions can lead to eternal treasure—revelations that can be learned only through the unexpected seasons that regularly come into our lives. The story of Joseph has all the elements of our own unexpected seasons—loss, waiting, renewal, redemption. As we look at the narrative together, we'll discover those principles nested into the plot—and we'll see how those principles inform our own perspective and the way we tell our stories. But first, let's dive into a little background on Joseph.

The Joseph Story

Several things about Joseph's story confound biblical scholars. Who is Joseph and why does it matter? Why is so much space given to his story when God is mentioned so little? Scholars disagree: Is he a conceited and naive teenager, rubbing his favored status in the face of his brothers? Or does Joseph deserve a more sympathetic reading, one that attributes Christlike virtue to his story? Once he becomes second-in-command to Pharaoh, are we to believe Joseph's prolonged testing of his brothers is some kind of cruel game designed to shame them into accepting his power, or does Joseph's hard-won wisdom make him shrewd in his approach to reconciling with them?

The Bible is frustratingly silent about Joseph's motivations, private thoughts, and outlook on his life. What's more, the story is pretty silent about God. There are no "God said to me" moments, no God-specific visions—even Joseph's dreams are quite rooted in the problems relevant to that day. Joseph doesn't experience any swooping imagery of angels or demons, of new heavens or Christ appearances. Some might say this ambiguity is a reason to let the story serve simply as a narrative to connect the dots in the big story of the Bible—a stopover that helps us understand how God's people got to Egypt so we can get on with the story of Moses.

Personally, I find the unknowns of the story refreshing. This ambiguity is what makes the story human, and when I take a closer look, the breathtaking humanity of it all shines through. In our opening scene, we see love and hate, envy and partiality, violence and compromise. We see humans doing what they do: Playing favorites. Getting mad. Speaking rashly. Making bad choices. Hurting people, even people they love.

Perhaps the overall lack of "God sightings" is an accurate picture of our lives, too, as we stumble through this dark and shadowy world. Of course, incredible things do happen in Joseph's life, but they unfold in an arc that spans months and years. They happen as Joseph stumbles along after being literally stripped of his most comfortable identity as favored son, discarded in an empty cistern, and sold for the price of a common slave. Before we get to the highlights, we must first engage the losses.

Loss: Universal *and* Personal

Loss is perhaps the most common experience that we all desperately want to avoid. What a strange thing it is to somehow believe that we might be the first human beings to avoid one of the most painful parts of our own humanity: losing something we love. Such a loss comes in many forms. It might be actual death—losing a person we love. But it might also be the loss of a relationship, the loss of a place, the loss of our sense of what the future will hold. Loss is somehow so universal yet so personal, and it comes to all of us. You can't buy or earn your way out of it; you can't guard yourself enough to avoid it. If you love anything or anyone, you will experience loss. And the only thing worse than the pain of loss is believing that you are isolated in it. And yet, when we turn to Scripture, we are surrounded by losses, by pain, by death and difficulty. They are as common as the sun rising and setting. So how, in our own lives, do we understand God's goodness in light of what feels so bad? Where is the fullness of life when we feel empty?

One gift that seems to be connected to middle age is the opportunity to hear and cherish stories from my peers who've experienced their own dramatic empty-ing as they were stripped of the relation-ships and identities most comfortable to them. The stories vary in circumstance but follow the same general arc: Favored status or comfortable identity is threatened by a series of unexpected losses that create painful exposure. Relationships that seemed unbreakable dissipate. Titles and positions, with the

> Loss is somehow so universal yet so personal, and it comes to all of us.

accompanying influence and security, disappear. It may be an un-expected diagnosis or accident; addiction; death; infidelity; sickness; unemployment; or waking up one day with a vague sense of not living into one's dream and no way to change the story. Loss comes in many forms.

Sometimes it comes suddenly, like the story I heard from someone who lost both their home and ranch in California wildfires. At other times, it unfolds gradually, like the many people who receive a cancer diagnosis, which is followed by uncertainty and pain during the long road of treatment and recovery. After we've sustained any challenge, we have to process what it means and how it impacts our dreams for the future. Sometimes this is the most difficult loss of all:

- The loss of confidence after our vocation takes a turn we didn't expect
- The loss of self-esteem after our sickness changes our appearance
- The loss of hope after a trusted friendship fizzles or explodes
- The loss of faith after our marriage ends or we lose a child
- The loss of purpose after we enter a new, unwanted stage of life
- The loss of freedom after we accept the restrictions of caregiving, our own limitations, or a lack of opportunities

Psychology has identified four types of grief that aren't connected to death:[2]

- Loss of identity—This comes when a role or connection that we had a strong emotional attachment to fails to continue. For instance, a retiree may experience the loss of significance and importance she felt for thirty years in her role as an elementary school teacher.

- Loss of safety—This happens when a physical, relational, sexual, or spiritual boundary is manipulated or violated. For instance, an experience of sexual abuse can make the whole world feel unsafe; a traumatic loss of relationships in church may lead someone to question their faith.

- Loss of autonomy—This is the inability to live and manage independently, either because someone depends on you or you must depend on another. For instance, you may lose independence when you become a parent for the first time or have a child with special needs. If you develop an illness or face a life situation that requires you to give up your own independence, you may also lose a sense of autonomy.

- Loss of dreams—Perhaps the most painful and misunderstood of all, the loss of dreams leads to confusion and pain from something—whether it's one's career, friendships, or relationship status—not working out as planned.

These losses are as significant as death to us, because in many ways, they are a death. We lose someone or something we love, even if that something is the dream we were holding on to about our own preferred future. With loss always comes grief—and it doesn't go away quietly.

Grief, Explained

Grief refuses to be linear. It's not a situation you can explain away or solve quickly. But naming loss and embracing grief as a part of the process can be the first healing step. With loss, what felt like a tough week easily turns into hard months with the slow realization that this *something* isn't a crisis; it's chronic. Rescue (at least as one might hope) isn't coming. Loss is a kind of dramatic emptying—like running at full sprint directly off a cliff. For Joseph, the first emptying and loss came when his brothers turned on him and threw him in a dry cistern—a literal pit. You may not be in a physical pit, but the idea of hitting rock bottom, of looking up from the base of a pit, might feel like an accurate metaphor of where this downward fall of loss and trial often takes us.

Yet following Joseph's swift and shocking emptying, his core identity remained. The test of loss simply revealed the character that was already there. Despite enduring the worst of human suffering, Joseph passed this test with flying colors. He lost it all but kept his faith. This testing, we realize, does something important: We often don't know who we really are—or who we are becoming—until everything we hold closest is lost. And here is where we find our first principle nested into the story of Joseph's loss: The test of loss is always an invitation to communion, to experience new levels of connection with God. Loss exposes us. And our grief—done well—invites us to a true knowledge of who we are, what we've come through, and what we need. It's in the very process of being emptied that true fulfillment with God can be discovered.

> We often don't know who we really are—or who we are becoming—until everything we hold closest is lost.

One of the hardest parts of grieving is knowing that no other human can fully understand what you are experiencing. But the best part of grieving is that God is not like anyone else. God is the One who can enter fully into your experience. He is the One who uses the test of loss to help you know Him better—and to know *yourself* better. That often starts with the lessons loss teaches us about who we are and where we've come from.

The Story of You

The poet T. S. Eliot wrote, "Home is where one starts from."[3] Like Joseph, your story is not just your story. It's generational, one in which the decisions you make are connected to the mothers and fathers of the past, and even more important—one that will connect to the people still to come.

It's taken me many years to connect to the stories that have gone before me. My mom left her home and upbringing in New York to marry my father and embrace the "great adventure" of the military lifestyle. But that lifestyle is quite nomadic and vaguely unsettling to the soul. To move every couple of years is to never quite settle anywhere. To this day, when people ask me where I'm from, I answer "nowhere" or "everywhere," depending on my outlook at the moment.

Military families are like tillandsia, those little plants that can exist without soil, feeding on miniscule nutrients and debris that hang in the air. Like those air plants, military families have dangling roots, neither connected to where they came from nor rooted in where they are going. (In reality, most air plants thrive by attaching themselves to other plants—a reminder that there is no such thing as a truly rootless existence. We all come from somewhere, whether we like it or not.)

The story of our own family often shapes our current emotional attachment. For instance, it doesn't take a PhD in psychology to realize that, though I once thought it was my now-husband Dave's winning smile that first attracted me to him, it was more likely his stable upbringing and steady personality that most appealed to me. After all, when I met him, I was desperate to have someplace and someone to call home. And I am overcome by the grace of God that our love was able to survive and grow beyond that immediate need in my young heart.

To this day, Dave is still my anchor and greatest place of "home"—but our emotional bond was first created because of the deep woundedness in my own story. Fast-forward twenty years, and that same deep need to find roots made losing our church home all the more painful. Regardless of the strength of the bond— disjointed, turbulent, loving, secure—we all have a connection to others, which will affect how we weather our unexpected seasons and the particular shape our stories take. All of us attach ourselves because that's what love does—and the greater the love, the greater the loss.

Wherever you are, whatever you are struggling with—you are not an island. Your story is intertwined with failures and victories from your mom and dad and your parents' parents. Regardless of whether your parents were involved, overinvolved, distant, detached, or completely disconnected from your life through abandonment, death, or addiction, and no matter how much time you spent with them, they are a part of you. Getting to know the stories of the generations before yours can ground you in what you will have to work to overcome as well as what you have to stand firmly upon.

And Joseph's experience was no different.

Joseph's fathers (and ours): Abraham, Isaac, Jacob

Just as we don't get to our real story without engaging deeply with the opening chapters in our own lives, so we don't get to the real and redeemed version of Joseph's story without considering the opening chapters of his life. So let's take a look at the key relationships that contributed both to his pain—and his faith.

Take Joseph's great-grandfather Abraham. You might know him as "the father of many nations" (Genesis 17:4). Despite a pretty miraculous experience of talking directly with God, Abraham still messed up. Not once but twice, he lied to powerful kings. He told them his beautiful wife, Sarah, was actually his sister because he was afraid these men would kill him to get to her. He took matters into his own hands again when it came to working around his wife's infertility to have a son, and that created generational conflict and strife. At ninety-nine, he laughed when Gold told him he would have a child in his old age. (Yes, his wife Sarah laughed at the thought too—but Genesis 17:17 tells us that Abraham laughed first.) The preposterous nature of a child born to a man and a woman who were both pushing one hundred was as crazy then as it sounds now. Given Abraham's tendency to lie and scheme, you might not immediately think that Abraham is the kind of man God would work through. And yet.

The Lord, in His faithfulness, declared to Abraham that through him an entire people group would fill the earth and that these people would be set apart to live in relationship with God. Abraham did the one right thing that mattered in God's eyes: He believed God. Despite his old age and in the face of an impossible situation, Abraham heard what God promised, and he trusted Him to deliver. And that was more than enough.

Years after Isaac, that miraculous child, was born, God tested Abraham by sending him up a mountain to sacrifice this one beloved son. We'll talk a lot more about testing in the next chapter, but it's important to remember that Abraham and Isaac went through some stuff—some hard stuff. Isaac would have remembered making the journey up the mountain with his father while carrying all the supplies they needed to sacrifice to God—everything, that is, except an actual sacrifice. When the altar was ready, God asked Abraham to give up Isaac, his only son, and this time Abraham's faith triumphed. In the face of an impossible, makes-no-sense command, Abraham trusted God. His belief in God's provision propelled his feet forward, and that belief became obedience in action. Just as Abraham moved to sacrifice Isaac, God spoke—He held back Abraham's hand and provided a ram for the sacrifice instead.

(Sidenote: Much later in the story of God's redemptive love, another Son would be offered as a sacrifice—Jesus, the only Son of God. But this time, God did not hold back His hand. He allowed Jesus to take the suffering of sin upon Himself so that the blessing that began in Abraham would carry on for thousands of years all the way to you and me. This ancient story isn't a myth designed to teach us a moral lesson. This is our history. This is our lineage, the story of a God who decides to show up, to bless His people, to provide.)

So now, Isaac lived the story, and he knew the stories. Like his father, Abraham, he was a man of faith. Yet also like his father, he did some pretty shady stuff. He pretended that his gorgeous wife was his sister to save his own neck. Isaac became the father of twins Esau and Jacob—and he made his favoritism known. "Isaac . . . loved Esau, but Rebekah loved Jacob" (Genesis 25:28). Jacob—the younger one, unfavored by his father—grew up in the dysfunction and deception of divided affections of his parents and the deceit that would haunt him into his adulthood.

Nonetheless, Jacob knew the stories of God's faithfulness too. And, yep, just like his father and his father before him, Jacob was a flawed (deeply flawed) human being. Let's start with the lowlights of Jacob's story, which read like a daytime soap opera or a nighttime reality show: Competitive and jealous of his brother, Jacob swindled Esau, taking his birthright for a bowl of stew. Basically, he stole his brother's inheritance. As if that weren't enough, Jacob, goaded on by his mother, conspired with her to steal the blessing that rightfully belonged to Esau by dressing up like him and tricking his almost-blind dad. Dirty.

As his life unfolded, Jacob was driven by his passions. When he saw a beautiful woman named Rachel for the first time, he kissed her and wept aloud (Genesis 29:11). After Jacob worked seven years for her hand in marriage, Laban, his father-in-law, gave him Rachel's older sister, Leah, at the wedding instead. (Listen, the bride was veiled, and there was a lot of drinking but no electricity. Strange things happened as a result.)

Laban rationalized his own trickery but eventually gave Rachel to Jacob too—after Jacob agreed to work another seven years for him. Now Jacob had sister wives who were jealous of one another. Once the kids started coming, their family's story basically turned into a soapy miniseries (you can read it for yourself in the second half of Genesis). Just like his uneven affection for his wives, Jacob played favorites with his children. He repeated the sins of his own family's favoritism with grave ramifications: a black pit of jealousy and bitterness between these twelve brothers of different mothers that ended with a torn robe, a cover-up, and a discarded teenager who became a slave.

Jacob was a master manipulator whose life was a mess he brought upon himself. But like his father and grandfather before him, he had this one thing going for him: He was a dreamer with a relationship with God. Before he met Rachel, he dreamed about a stairway to heaven in which God reaffirmed His promise about his descendants (Genesis 28:10-17)—the promise God had given Jacob's dad, Isaac, and granddad Abraham. Later, while laboring for Laban, Jacob had a dream about goat breeding, a warning that things were going south with his father-in-law (Genesis 31:10-12).

But most notably, during a long and dreamless night, Jacob grappled with God. An angel of the Lord appeared to him as a man, and they wrestled all night. In the morning, Jacob, with the strength of someone who was desperately trying to figure out who he was, refused to let the mysterious figure go without a blessing (Genesis 32:22-32). Jacob later realized that this supernatural wrestling match was an encounter with the living God. He left that encounter with a limp and a new name, Israel—and he left a changed man.

When God called Jacob to settle in Bethel, Jacob announced this plan to his children, saying God is the one "who answered me in the day of my distress and who has been with me wherever I have gone" (Genesis 35:3). This was the statement of a man who'd become something despite his ongoing patterns of manipulation and passions. These were the words of one who didn't just know *of* God but who practiced *knowing* God.

Jacob told his sons about this God. His favorite son, Joseph, knew the stories of his own flawed but loving father. He would know about his grandfather Isaac, who experienced the God who provides deliverance; he would know the stories of his great-grandfather Abraham, who experienced God as the one who blesses. Although these ancient stories may seem far removed from our everyday struggles, God's ongoing interaction and good intentions for His children are the same today.

This is a God who is with us.

Joseph—in the bottom of that pit, through the dark days that followed being sold into slavery, stripped of his identity and security—still had *this*. He had stories. He had his memory. He had the knowledge of a faithful God who ultimately comes through.

Joseph had the story of Abraham. He knew that God interrupts our existence with His presence and meets us face-to-face. He knew God continues to bless us despite our failings.

Joseph had the story of Isaac. He knew that God provides even when it seems like there is no way out.

Joseph had the story of Jacob. He knew that God understands our patterns of deceit and that blessing sometimes comes only by wrestling for it.

Each of us also has a story. We have early chapters in those stories—for better and for worse. We have the circumstances that have shaped us. We have the needs that have tempted us to find the source of our belonging and love in people, places, and achievements. And we have our losses—the grief we may be feeling right now, whether it's fresh in this season or something we've been trying to find meaning in for decades.

Like us, Joseph had both the good and the bad from his family. And even though he'd lost everything—his family, his home, his culture, his identity—nothing could take away his memory—his understanding of the God whose power and presence have no boundaries.

In order to understand what Joseph lost, we have to understand what he had. Joseph's own story—and ours—always starts in the middle of someone else's story. God can be good, but our sin—and the sin of our fathers and mothers—still has consequences. Pain is never experienced in a vacuum. The way we experience pain, cope with pain, and frame pain in our lives impacts the people around us. Jacob coped with the struggles with his wives by playing favorites with his sons. His heart was wrapped up in his two youngest sons because they were a reminder of his beloved wife, Rachel, but that had consequences. His open affection for Joseph and Benjamin came at the cost of their other ten older brothers. Look at how Jacob (named Israel) impacts the story of his sons:

> *Now Israel loved Joseph more than any of his other sons . . .*
> *and he made an ornate robe for him. When his brothers*
> *saw that their father loved him more than any of them,*
> *they hated him and could not speak a kind word to him.*
> GENESIS 37:3-4

Joseph's brothers hated him, could not speak a kind word to him. But somehow Joseph didn't seem to notice—or mind. Secure in his relationship and standing with his father, he spoke freely of the misdeeds of several of his brothers: "He brought their father a bad report about them" (Genesis 37:2). And he had no problem sharing dreams God gave him: "Joseph had a dream, and when he told it to his brothers, they hated him all the more" (verse 5).

Joseph had what they all wanted—to be favored by their father; to be loved; to be noticed. Perhaps Joseph's security with his father created a naiveté in him, an inability to see how his wide-open sharing of dreams that his brothers would bow down to him would ignite the violent jealously lurking under the surface. Perhaps he would have been more careful if he had been more aware—but that's the thing about attaching ourselves to a status or identity. We don't see how much it matters to us until it's gone.

Then one day Joseph was sent (again) to check on his brothers. But this time, they didn't wait around for him to return to their father with a bad report. This time, they ambushed him: "Come now, let's kill him. . . . Then we'll see what comes of his dreams" (Genesis 37:20).

Never Forsaken

Often our own pain is the result of someone's suffering before us. We are misunderstood or ignored as kids because of the pain our own parents are experiencing. We are passed over or rejected because of the pain that keeps someone we want to please from noticing us. When someone battling pain from their past collides with us and our needs, the shrapnel wounds us all.

Unfortunately, some of us can relate all too well to this part of the story. We've experienced intentional harm from those who were supposed to cherish, protect, and believe in us. The story of Joseph's mistreatment and abandonment is familiar. Or we may not have experienced outright violence to our bodies, but we understand betrayal in our hearts. We know what it feels like to trust someone, to believe in someone, or to love someone, only to be betrayed. We know the deepest kind of pain that comes when we feel abandoned or devalued by someone we trusted with our full selves. For all of us who are willing to enter Joseph's story, we relate to the start of his unexpected season. We know what it's like to have a familiar role or identity lost or taken away, and then to feel abandoned and forsaken, just as Joseph was left in the bottom of a cistern.

Friend, I don't know the circumstances of your unexpected season, but I do know how disorienting these times are. We feel helpless and unsure of how to move forward. We feel so lost. Should we retrace our steps or just forge ahead? Should we hang on to anything from the past? We feel alone and unsteady, but we move forward anyway. We have to. We get up in the morning, we brush our teeth, we do the dishes. Throughout the day, and often at the most inconvenient times, we may feel the waves of overwhelm threatening to knock us out. When we feel the tears, anger, or anxiety well up within us, we press them down and press on. We keep moving forward even when it feels like everything is falling apart. And all along, God is still writing a story. God is still working with intention. God is still as near as the tears in your eyes.

In Joseph's hour of darkness, in the tenderness of his bruises, in the pain pooling in the tears in his eyes, and in the questions of his heart—God was still near. Whether he believed it or not—God was still near. There is so much pain in loss, and the deepest of all is the feeling of being left without the person, place, position, or idea you've held so closely to your heart. Maybe this is why I'm attracted to the idea of God showing up in so many forms: the mysterious figure that Jacob wrestled with; the strange figure in the furnace with Shadrach, Meshach, and Abednego;[4] and the person of Jesus, who came humbly, unassumingly, and without fanfare into the world and into our hearts. It's a reminder that even at my most alone, God is still *El Roi*, the God who sees me.[5] And even at your most alone, God is still the One who sees you. Jesus came into the world and experienced all the pain the world had to give so that no matter what loss we experience, we never have to lose communion with God. No matter how hard your own family story is, no matter how searing the loss, no matter how gutted or angry or numb or lost you feel, you never travel your story alone.

In C. S. Lewis's *The Horse and His Boy*, the young boy Shasta runs away to avoid being sold as a slave. As he makes his frightening journey alone, Shasta realizes that someone or something mighty is traveling unseen beside him. When this creature invites Shasta to tell him his woes, Shasta talks about a frightening lion that chased him the night before:

Aslan responds, "I was the lion."

And as Shasta gapes at him and says nothing, the voice continues:

I was the lion who forced you to join with Aravis. I was the cat who comforted you among the houses of the dead. I was the lion who drove the jackals from you while you slept. I was the lion who gave the Horses the new strength of fear for the last mile so that you should reach King Lune in time. And I was the lion you do not remember who pushed the boat in which you lay, a child near death, so that it came to shore where a man sat, wakeful at midnight, to receive you.[6]

What would it be like to look back on this season and know that God was always with you? That in the pain, in the emptying, the stripping away of everything that mattered to you, *He* was always there, guiding, moving, providing, and redeeming it all?

What if in the mystery of how God redeems all things, He can be with you and near you in the pain of yesterday, the pain of today, even the inevitable pain that you'll face tomorrow? What if, even in the pain, even in the struggle, even in the unanswered questions and ongoing doubts, He is still *with* you, He is still *for* you, and He still *intends good*?

A PRAYER FROM THE PIT

God,

So You promise that all of this can work together
    for good.
But the view from down here is so dark, and I am
    so empty.
It's hard to breathe,
much less hope.

You're right—I'm finding out a lot about me.
Turns out I'm desperate, and worried, and angry,
    and sad.

You say through this I can become something new.
You say You'll provide comfort,
and rescue,
and even redemption?

Well, I can't see anything in this darkness.
So I'll just have to trust in what You can see,
and who You say I am,
and where this is going—as long as You go with me.

Amen (I guess).

Now Joseph was well-built and handsome, and after a while his master's wife took notice of Joseph and said, "Come to bed with me!"

But he refused. "With me in charge," he told her, "my master does not concern himself with anything in the house; everything he owns he has entrusted to my care. No one is greater in this house than I am. My master has withheld nothing from me except you, because you are his wife. How then could I do such a wicked thing and sin against God?"

GENESIS 39:6-9

CHAPTER 4

THE TEST OF INTEGRITY

*One of the truest tests of integrity is its
blunt refusal to be compromised.*

CHINUA ACHEBE

If you've ever taken your life into your own hands on a carnival
ride, you may have encountered that particular brand of torture
commonly called the Gravitron—also known as the "throw-up
machine." You, along with maybe a dozen other people, enter a
stuffy, circular, flying saucer–like contraption padded with mats.
You each stand against one of the curved walls. There are no seat
belts, latches, or safety bars to pull down. Truly, there are no rules
of any kind. Once everyone is in place, the ride begins to whir
and beep, slowly spinning and turning faster with each rotation as
neon strobe lights flash and club music plays at deafening volumes.
The spinning, the lights, and general cacophony evoke the feeling
of simultaneously losing control of both body and mind. These
three minutes of "entertainment" are what I imagine it would be
like if you were being rocketed into space while being spun in a
washing machine.

It's a real joy. Make sure you check it out the next time you want to spend an exorbitant amount of money to potentially terrorize yourself or your children. That feeling though—the result of the spinning, the music, and the forces assaulting your body—is not unlike the way we experience the world today. We somehow must hold together opposing forces. Yes, God created and controls the still waters and roaring seas; yes, Jesus has overcome the world; and also yes, the forces of good and evil still wage little skirmishes and bloody battles in our souls.

This contradictory reality of being held by an all-powerful God even as we live in a world where good and evil are always at war leads to conflict. Being "pulled apart" works against our *integrity*, a word defined as "an undivided or unbroken completeness."[1] To have integrity is to have wholeness—a mind, heart, and body aligned and moving toward the same purpose.

In other words, a person of integrity has strong moral principles and behaves in accordance with those principles, even when it hurts. *Integrity is intention in action.* Just about everyone believes they have integrity; no one wants to admit that they struggle with this virtue. But in reality, we all fail at integrity. The unseen forces in our world are constantly working to pull apart that which we so desperately want to keep together.

The test of integrity naturally follows the test of loss. Integrity is always about matters at the rock bottom of who we are, examined when things we love are stripped away. We enter deeply into our own reality when we face unexpected seasons. We have to confront the truth of who we really are, what we really care about, how we are really doing. All of this "reality" can be difficult to manage, but the test of integrity is also an invitation to discover clarity, which comes when our comfortable identity feels stripped away, and what we value most and who we really are surface.

Integrity is intention in action.

When life goes according to plan, it's easy to stay aligned with our values. But when things go sideways or backwards or spin out of control—when it feels as if our lives have been tossed into the Gravitron—we face tests of integrity that may challenge us like never before. We are tempted to take shortcuts as an attempt to rush past uncomfortable losses, insecurities, and shortcomings. In our pain we often discover weaknesses and vulnerabilities that we've managed to cover up in the past and that now demand our energy. How we handle—and satisfy—those needs is the challenge ahead.

Yet even when all seems lost in our story, we still have so much—as we'll discover in Joseph's life. After being sold into slavery by his brothers, he found himself in the household of a high-ranking Egyptian official. Faced with staggering losses, Joseph was about to be tempted with his own test of integrity, which would change the trajectory of his young life.

The Prospering of Joseph

We left Joseph in a true pit. Stripped of his coat and thrown in a cistern, Joseph was defenseless. Fortunately, his brothers deviated from their original plan to kill him in their jealousy and hatred; instead, they sold him to some Midianite traders riding by. We can only imagine what Joseph's journey to Egypt must have been like, but it had to have been both terrifying and brutal. Once there, Joseph was sold to a captain of the guard named Potiphar—one of Pharaoh's officials. What happens next is a powerful picture of God's presence:

> *The LORD was with Joseph so that he prospered, and he lived in the house of his Egyptian master. When his master saw that the LORD was with him and that the LORD gave him success in everything he did, Joseph found favor in his eyes and became his attendant. Potiphar put him in charge of his household, and he entrusted to his care everything he*

owned. From the time he put him in charge of his household
and of all that he owned, the LORD blessed the household
of the Egyptian because of Joseph. The blessing of the LORD
was on everything Potiphar had, both in the house and in
the field.

GENESIS 39:2-5

Notice that the words *prosper, favor, success,* and *blessing* are emphasized repeatedly in this chapter of Joseph's life. But Joseph was still very much a slave. He was not his own. He was young and defenseless and still suffering from great loss—rejection, abandonment, betrayal. He was in an unknown land with no power and no family. I would say that for God to call this a blessing is a stretch—unless, of course, His idea of blessing is quite different from our own. Remember God's promise we laid out in chapter 2? God has plans to accomplish good *for* you and *through* you. We see this type of blessing early in Genesis through the story of Abram (whose name is later changed by God to Abraham), where blessing meant something that would benefit not only Abram but countless others through him: "All peoples on earth will be blessed through you" (Genesis 12:3). When God promises to prosper you, it's never about your comfort or wealth or success for your sake alone—it's always for the sake of what can happen through you.

Many Christians are confused about what the blessing of salvation—or God's blessings in general—looks like in their lives. Because we are steeped in a culture that promises a dream quite different from the kind we find in the Bible, we may find ourselves mixing up or intertwining the two.

When people today say they are blessed, they generally mean they are experiencing financial wealth or good health, or are successful in their work or parenting. They may mean that they can take a vacation this year or that no one they love is sick, dying, or messing up. This is actually the definition of the American dream, which is defined as a "national ethos . . . in which freedom is interpreted as the opportunity for individual prosperity and success."[2] The American dream is not just American though. It's built upon the promise that if we work hard enough, we will get ahead and provide wealth and ease for ourselves and our children. And it's easy to believe that this cultural reality is also a spiritual reality—that God must mean comfort and ease when He talks about blessing and prosperity.

God *may* include these comforts in His dream for us, but His intention for us is most certainly not defined by them. The blessing of our salvation is an invitation to live right now in the kingdom of God, a place of "righteousness, peace and joy" (Romans 14:17). We carry the kingdom of heaven with us wherever we go, creating something like a kingdom force field that impacts everyone we influence. While the kingdom of this world operates like a Gravitron that seems to be frantically trying to pull us apart, the kingdom of heaven is the opposite, a place of shalom, that peace that gently invites us—and everyone around us—to be reconciled and whole.

God is as faithful today as He was when He gave the promise to Abram, a promise that continued forward to Isaac and Jacob and carries forward as spiritual DNA to everyone who calls themselves followers of Jesus. But because our understanding of blessing may have been corrupted, we may find ourselves confused, ashamed, or angry when what we call "blessings" don't seem to show up in our lives or are stripped away during seasons of loss. *Prosper, favor, success,* and *blessing* might be the words used to describe Joseph's situation in the house of Potiphar, but anyone walking down the streets of Egypt and observing Joseph wouldn't have called him blessed.

And yet the story repeatedly emphasizes that in this exile and place of pain, Joseph was prospering. The way Joseph lived, worked, and engaged with others was visible to Potiphar. As Joseph's integrity and intelligence became known, Potiphar trusted him with more and more—until he put everything he owned in

Joseph's care. In other words, being blessed in this case was not as much about Joseph's happiness as it was about Potiphar's! And although we don't know how or if God directly interacted with Joseph, Scripture is very clear that Potiphar experienced blessings only because God was showing His favor to and through Joseph. God calls this chapter of Joseph's story blessed, not cursed.

Bitter Blessings

So with this in mind, we learn that blessing is not just good for the sake of you—in fact, it might not feel good for you at all. But God has good He intends to disperse *through* you. And sometimes it's in the midst of our own pit or prison season that others are blessed through us.

I watched this play out after my dear friends Stacie and JR had their second child on August 13, 2022. This beautiful baby girl, Mollie, was born full term, but she then experienced one traumatic event after another. She had to be given CPR at birth after a sudden cord prolapse. She was then sedated and placed in a medically induced hypothermia (a procedure in which her whole body was cooled to protect her brain) for three days. On the day she was meant to go home, she caught a common virus that wracked her already-weakened body and attacked her heart. On that same day, she was transferred by ambulance from one hospital to another while a team of medical experts stood over her, manually pressing air into her lungs as she clung to life by a spider's thread.

The shock of each day of bad news culminated in this moment, when Stacie called in sobs. She and JR had been told to say goodbye to Mollie in case she didn't survive the short ambulance ride to a hospital that *might* be able to sustain her life. I had preached out of state that morning, so I pressed my foot to the accelerator and willed my car to get back home as fast as possible.

Once at the hospital, I circled the building, trying in my own confused and anxious haze to find an unlocked door. Minutes later, I watched the ambulance transporting baby Mollie from the suburban hospital pull up, with her parents behind in their car. I'll never forget the next moment, looking across the downtown intersection on a beautiful, sunny summer day—a day on which many people were lounging by the pool or grilling out with friends—as these two young parents exited the car, facing their worst nightmare. Stacie and I are so close that I consider her more like a sister than a friend. We have the kind of friendship in which we easily laugh with, cry with, sit quietly with, shop with, and make food with each other. She is also my closest ministry partner—the one I had depended on to hold my life together. Now she walked toward me, a picture of a life coming apart. Her face was slack, her eyes empty, and her belly still swollen from birth. As we embraced, I held her as tightly as I could, trying to do the impossible—relieve some of the pain, provide an anchor. In moments like these, when everything seems to be falling apart, we try to be held or hold on tightly enough to stop the Gravitron from pulling us apart. We cling to one another as a reverse force against that which threatens to ravage us with grief. *This place of devastating loss is not what Stacie, JR, or I would call a blessing.*

But yet. In the weeks that followed, the shimmer and glimmer of God's goodness—yes, dare I say, God's blessing—showed up in Mollie's story. I saw it in the hundreds of believers who purposefully and passionately prayed for Mollie's heart—they were blessed through her. God's blessing was in the nurses and doctors who gave all of their intellect, experience, and creativity to try a dozen different ways to heal Mollie's heart—they were blessed through her. The medical technicians, the ministry providing an apartment for Mollie's parents, and the caregivers watching Mollie's big brother, Gibson, were blessed. Blessings can come in painful packages, and those circumstances don't take away the fact that they are blessings. In fact, painful and unexpected seasons correct our bad theology around what God sometimes calls "good." Stacie, JR, and baby Mollie suffered mightily—and yet there was still good.

Blessing looks like this message Stacie received, a few weeks after a procedure that was one of the inch-by-inch miracles that have sustained Mollie's life:

> Dear Stacie, you don't know me, but I saw a post from Third Church about Mollie. I recognized the story—I'm a nurse at VCU and was in the lab where they did the surgery to put a "helpful hole" in her heart. . . . I just wanted you to know that I prayed for her before her procedure. I also prayed for "Mollie's parents" that God would meet you in this particular valley. . . . I mostly wanted to message you to be another testimony to how God is caring for you & Mollie—the church body is all around you guys, city to city, and even (unknowingly) right in the procedure room with your baby girl. God is so good & His people are faithful.

I've found that when I'm living in the midst of a dark season, it is easier to recognize God's faithfulness when I look outward rather than inward. Rather than fixating on my own turmoil, when I witness God working in other's lives, I'm reminded that my story isn't finished yet.

The first Easter after I'd left my role on a church staff also happened to be the first Easter of the pandemic. Easter had always been my favorite time on staff—an occasion when our creativity, teamwork, and messaging came to its greatest apex. The Easter I'd anticipated feeling the most nostalgia and loss turned out to be a different Easter altogether, as it did for the world. Our whole life had slowed down; our family had recentered itself (for better or for worse). I was facing my own shift in identity, a loss of belonging, and my uncertain future—but I was also seeing new sides of my children and husband as we all weathered the pandemic together. I wrote a long entry in my journal that day: "It's a beautiful Easter day, and the sun is still shining. . . ." I went on to capture all the good I saw coming out of my kids in that season. Instead of experiencing firsthand the great pivot churches had to face in 2020, I was just capturing the small pivots in my own family's life. And somehow rehearsing the goodness of God despite my pain made it a little more palatable.

No doubt Joseph, too, recognized shimmers of God's faithfulness as he prospered in his role, as he showed up faithfully and with integrity to do what God placed in front of him. In your own dark seasons, God's blessing probably won't be what you thought it would be, but that doesn't mean you can't prosper in it.

The Real Housewives of Egypt

What happens next in Joseph's story is nothing short of a Bravo reality show, complete with lies, sex, and conspiracy. (PS If you are uncomfortable with the reality of how humans really behave, you will be uncomfortable with the Bible.) But remember the invitation from chapter 1? We are not about skipping and stuffing it while creating a superficial world where we can pretend that bad things don't happen. We want to live into the real and redeemed story that God has for each one of us—and along the way, we will face tests of integrity that can be either obstacles or opportunities.

For Joseph, that test came in the form of a wealthy wife caught up in . . . something. It's easy to immediately assume Potiphar's wife was motivated by desire when she noticed that Joseph was "well-built and handsome." Or maybe she was bored, as her husband "did not concern himself with anything except the food he ate" (Genesis 39:6). That's not exactly a recipe for a spicy and fulfilling marriage. Maybe Potiphar's wife desired children, and since many of Pharaoh's officials were eunuchs,[3] it's possible she wanted to use Joseph to have a child. We don't know her motivation, but we do know that she had power—and she was persistent. Time and time again she propositioned Joseph, who would be around a lot since he was functioning as head of the household and making sure everything was in order.

As if the plot was written for reality TV, the tension came to a boiling point when Potiphar's wife found an opportune moment alone with Joseph and grabbed hold of his cloak, crying, "Come to bed with me!" (Genesis 39:12). But in his eagerness to get out of the situation, Joseph slipped out of his cloak to get away from her grasp. Though we don't know exactly what motivated Potiphar's wife to come after Joseph the way she did, we do know that she responded as we might expect someone who is not used to being told no. She got mad. And she got even. "This Hebrew has been brought to us to make sport of us!" (verse 14), she told everyone who would listen. After all, she had his cloak as proof.

When her husband came home, she repeated the lie: "This is how your slave treated me" (verse 19). In my mind, I hear her do what couples often do in distress: They blame. "This is how *your* slave treated *me*." This is *your* doing, and it's impacted *me*. Potiphar burned with anger, but apparently not enough fury to subject Joseph to the standard sentence for adultery back then— execution.[4] Perhaps Potiphar burned with anger not just against Joseph but against his wife, against the situation, and against the loss of his most trusted servant who had made life so easy for him. And despite behaving with integrity—making the only right choice in this situation—Joseph was not rewarded; he was punished. And once again, he was stripped of his cloak and all that it represented and was again unjustly thrown into a pit—this time, the king's prison.

This is a reminder that doing the right thing is often hard, and it may not get you recognition at all—in fact, it might make things worse! But doing the right thing in order to elicit praise or acceptance is not integrity; it's manipulation. Integrity is intention in action—no matter the consequences. And in Joseph's case, integrity landed him right back in what must have felt like a terrible rerun of his past pain.

As Joseph fended off temptation again and again, we see his character tested. Testing is a strange position to be in because it may appear to us that God is setting us up to fail. But God does not test us to tempt us. Scripture is very clear on this point:

> *When tempted, no one should say, "God is tempting me." For God cannot be tempted by evil, nor does he tempt anyone; but each person is tempted when they are dragged away by their own evil desire and enticed.*
>
> JAMES 1:13-14

Testing is not about God trying to see if we will falter or fail. Testing is about revealing what God already knows is in our hearts.

Why Tests?

Whether your test comes in the form of an aggressive proposition, like Joseph's, or in a much subtler form, like trying to make it through the T.J. Maxx checkout line without impulse buying Thanksgiving decorations and dog toys, tests of integrity are all around us. *God tests us to reveal what is already there.*

My kids attend a high school that draws from several different counties. Because the students come from such a variety of backgrounds, most freshman year classes include pretests or placement tests. Even though my kids were told repeatedly that the placement tests are not something you "pass" or "fail," they were anxious when they took them because there were some questions they just couldn't answer. When it comes to tests of character, we might feel the same way. Even though we've learned that we are works in progress, that we are saved by faith, and that God is never done with us, when we fail miserably at a test of our character, we may wonder if that offer has an expiration date. It's easy to believe that when we fail a test of our integrity, God might be done with us. Our failing may also make us feel more shame about the loss we've experienced. But tests of integrity, particularly in our "not what I signed up for" seasons, are opportunities to learn—and clarify—who we really are.

God does not play hide-and-seek when it comes to these tests. He uses this time to reveal to us what is in our hearts: who we are becoming and what we are believing. Here are three reasons that testing in our unexpected seasons can be a good thing:

Tests teach us to fear God

Tests give us a proper understanding of God's holiness and the ramifications of sin. In Exodus 20, the Israelites drew back in fear as God appeared in fire and lightning on Mount Sinai. Moses told the people: "Do not be afraid. God has come to test you, so that the fear of God will be with you to keep you from sinning" (verse 20).

This "fear of God" is a reverent and respectful awe meant to inform our actions. Even if we love the ocean, we can also "fear the ocean." When we have a proper understanding of the power of currents, sharks, and riptides, we act accordingly. When God comes near His people, terror generally ensues. Whenever humans get close to the sheer holiness and majesty of who He actually is, they freak out. No wonder that most God-encounters begin with a divine agent—whether an angel or God Himself—saying, "Do not be afraid."

Jesus says the same to us today. After telling His followers not to worry about their everyday needs, He added, "Do not be afraid, little flock, for your Father has been pleased to give you the kingdom" (Luke 12:32). He told His disciples "Do not be afraid" when they panicked after seeing Him walk on water toward their boat during a furious storm (Matthew 14:27, esv). He told those praising Him as He came into Jerusalem—where He would be crucified days later—"Do not be afraid . . . your king is coming"

(John 12:15). Only when we bow before His presence, aware of His power and holiness, can we accept His outstretched hand of comfort and courage: Do not be afraid.

The fear of God is always good when it leads us to a proper understanding of His sovereignty and power. The fear of God is good when it leads us to say, like Joseph, "Am I in the place of God?" (Genesis 50:19). Knowing that God uses struggle to increase our faith and make us more like Jesus allows us to interpret our unexpected seasons from a different perspective.

Tests reveal what God already knows is in our hearts

You might want to read that again. God tests us to show us what He already knows is in our hearts. God does not test us to get information about our thoughts and attitudes. He knows all the days of our lives (Psalm 139:16). He knows every hair on our heads (Matthew 10:30). Jesus reveals that He knows "what [is] in each person's heart" (John 2:25, NLT). So clearly God is never testing us for His revelation—His testing is for our revelation.

I find that most of the time, I fail these tests mightily. When I'm tested, I'm much more prone to recognize my broken integrity than to celebrate how whole and at peace I am. One recent night before I was scheduled to preach the next morning, I lay awake in my bed, wracked with shame. I found myself rehearsing all the ways I wasn't fit to be a pastor—wasn't holy enough or disciplined enough or just plain good enough to get up and address people. I tossed and turned most of the night, alternately fretting about the state of my soul and lamenting about how bad my sermon was going to be the next morning. At one point, tears fell from my eyes as I laid my head down on my arm and willed sleep to come.

It was a moment of utter dejection—a complete emptying of any sense that I was called, capable, or qualified. I think my soul took one last death shudder as I gave up any sense of my own independent worth or self-created righteousness. And in that moment, I experienced a profound sense of acceptance and unconditional love that I can hardly put into words. It was a warmth, it was a color, it was a presence, it was a gift. In the moment that I had the greatest sense of my own emptiness, a presence of love was there to fill it.

Testing is sometimes about making the right choice, about shrugging out of the cloak, about keeping your integrity by giving up something good or comfortable. But testing can also reveal who you really are so you become real enough to meet God for who He really is—merciful, loving, patient, kind.

Tests reposition our hearts toward God

Before my restless night of wrestling about my worth, I would have told you that my heart was positioned for receiving from God. But it was only when I was truly emptied that I could completely surrender myself to His mercy and grace. God provides tests that allow us to discover—and reposition—our hearts toward Him. King David, when bringing gifts to God on behalf of the Israelites, named the most real position our hearts can ever attain: "I know, my God, that you test the heart and are pleased with integrity. All these things I have given willingly and with honest intent" (1 Chronicles 29:17).

Given willingly. God, I've done my best to bring You who I am, the real me. *And with honest intent.* God, I've searched my deceptive heart; I've traced the borders of my chronic insecurity; I've plumbed the depths of my fear. I've done the best with exactly who I am, and that person is not perfect, is not sinless, and most certainly does not emerge victorious from every test and trial. Giving willingly and with honest intent *is* integrity.

In seasons of loss and in checks of integrity, we discover not only who we are becoming but what we are believing.

What We Are Believing

When Joseph rebuffed Potiphar's wife, he revealed the belief system that motivated him during his long years of servitude and isolation. Historical research indicates that extramarital relationships were likely very common—even encouraged—in ancient Egypt.[5] But that didn't deter Joseph from responding with integrity to this woman's advances. His rationale went like this:

> *My master does not concern himself with anything in the house; everything he owns he has entrusted to my care. No one is greater in this house than I am. My master has withheld nothing from me except you, because you are his wife. How then could I do such a wicked thing and sin against God?*
>
> GENESIS 39:8-9

In one short statement, Joseph revealed his beliefs about trust and morality. Trust is built by being a person of boundaries, one who considers the ramifications of their choices. Even more important, Joseph connected his choices to his relationship with God. It's very similar to the way David responded when confronted by the prophet Nathan about his violent sexual sin against Bathsheba and successful plot to arrange for her husband Uriah's death (like I said, don't come to the Bible if you are uncomfortable with humanity). When Nathan brought up David's misdeeds, David immediately responded: "I have sinned against the LORD" (2 Samuel 12:13).

Considering how God may be testing your integrity may seem like a strange thing to do during your unexpected season. But this is precisely the right time to think about it. When you feel stuck, weary, or wounded, you are also fragile and more likely to believe that you are responsible for the mess you're in, so you should probably give up on trusting God anyway. It's in seasons like this when it absolutely feels better to hold on to anger, vengeance, or self-hatred than to trust a good God.

We are tempted to take this kind of shortcut when our losses are real and our comforts and security have been stripped away. The first shortcut we can take is to skip and stuff: to avoid bringing our real selves to God and to pretend like all is okay while perhaps secretly numbing our pain with any pleasure we can find. Or maybe the shortcut we take is to dive and dwell into those feelings, nursing our pain and fantasies of vengeance, sinking into our painful shame story without the redemptive hope and healing presence of God.

Despite the temptation he must have felt, Joseph understood that there is no such thing as a harmless sin. Despite pressure day after day, he resisted and then fled the temptation posed by one determined and unhappy woman. How does a person have the strength to make the hard choice? It comes from a vision for life that goes beyond the moment of testing. Joseph may have lost his family identity, his community, his language, his culture, and his place to worship; but what he still had was a dream, and he still had his stories. What he carried with him is the one thing you can also carry—specifically, the integrity that is rooted in the story of God's love in your life, the faith of those who have gone before you. Even in the worst unexpected season, if you still have integrity, you still have everything. And sometimes it's only in the pain of loss that we can discover with clarity what truly matters to us: the source of our integrity, the values we hold, the person we want to become. It doesn't happen quickly. It usually comes after several failed attempts. But the test of integrity brings a gift: an invitation to clarity.

> When things you value are taken away or when you have to walk away to hold on to your integrity, you are being given opportunities.

Joseph's story started with a beautiful robe being stripped away. Our chapter ends with a cloak being given away. Tests of loss and integrity: When things you value are taken away or when you have to walk away to hold on to your integrity, you are being given opportunities. You have the chance to discover, maybe painfully, who you really are and who you are becoming. And you are invited to fall on the mercy of God, the One to whom you can always say: "I am always with you; you hold me by my right hand" (Psalm 73:23).

A PRAYER TO REST

Lord,

I know that when I rest, I trust.
Allow me to surrender the burdens of the past,
the worries for the future, and the anxiety of the
  moment into Your care,
at least for one day.
Give me the clarity to see that even when all else
  seems to fail, including me,
there is no greater gift than to be loved by You.

Thank You for reminding me that it often takes
  more faith to rest
than it does to act.

Amen.

When his master heard the story his wife told him, saying, "This is how your slave treated me," he burned with anger. Joseph's master took him and put him in prison, the place where the king's prisoners were confined. . . .

After they had been in custody for some time, each of the two men—the cupbearer and the baker of the king of Egypt, who were being held in prison—had a dream the same night, and each dream had a meaning of its own.

When Joseph came to them the next morning, he saw that they were dejected. So he asked Pharaoh's officials who were in custody with him in his master's house, "Why do you look so sad today?"

"We both had dreams," they answered, "but there is no one to interpret them."

Then Joseph said to them, "Do not interpretations belong to God? Tell me your dreams. . . .

"But when all goes well with you, remember me and show me kindness; mention me to Pharaoh and get me out of this prison. I was forcibly carried off from the land of the Hebrews, and even here I have done nothing to deserve being put in a dungeon."

GENESIS 39:19-20; 40:4-8, 14-15

CHAPTER 5

THE TEST OF HUMILITY

Humility is throwing oneself away in complete
concentration on something or someone else.

MADELEINE L'ENGLE, *A CIRCLE OF QUIET*

It took me longer than most people to realize that I couldn't be successful enough or perfect enough to get out of humbling experiences. I held on to the lie that somehow I was smart enough to avoid suffering; that when others were rejected, passed over, or pushed aside, there must have been something they could have done to avoid it. My parents raised me with the mentality that there's always a way to make something happen: If you get creative enough and pray enough and—for sure—if you work hard enough, it will go well for you. And although on the whole I'm glad I was raised to pioneer, it did mean I had a steep slope to descend when I began to realize life doesn't always work that way.

I remember the specific moment when I realized I had not been chosen to fill a position I'd been excited about for years. I believed the person selected was less experienced, less educated, and less skilled than me, so I could discern no reason I was passed over for this role. I did a searching inventory on my own pride (wounded), examined my own performance and feedback I'd received to try to understand the decision (I couldn't). I began to spiral, first into embarrassment and then anger. I constructed an imaginary courtroom in my mind where I could prosecute everyone standing against me—my boss, my leaders, the world in general. I rapidly cycled through so many emotions before realizing what I was experiencing most deeply was disillusionment—my deep-seated belief that I could work hard enough to control every outcome had been shattered.

I had three choices: I could continue to blame others for my misery and allow the fast-growing weed of bitterness to take root and begin to poison my soul. I could blame myself and heap more shame upon my own head, leaning into my workaholic tendencies even more. Or I could take the third way—the way of humility. To be fair, I ping-ponged between the first two choices for months after this moment. Okay, I ping-ponged for years. The heart is a deceitful thing. We make progress one day, regress the next. But what I've come to understand is that these experiences can be a gift that can actually lead to freedom—a painful but necessary deconstruction of inaccurate beliefs about ourselves, our God, and the world.

But here's the rub: There is nothing more slippery to grab on to or more difficult to measure than humility. When you are struggling through an unexpected season, examining your humility feels like a fool's errand. After all, as you attend to your real and present needs during a period of loss, anger, or grief, taking time to ask whether you truly understand humility sounds almost laughable.

Yet what if humility is not only a virtue God loves, but also the number one survival tactic for unexpected seasons? When a rogue wave of life catches you unaware and off guard, you are *already* doing your best to just hold it together. That is precisely the point: *Humility is about letting go of holding it together so you can release it into God's hands.*

Humility is about rightsizing your expectations about who you are and how you show up in the world. But humility is not self-condemnation—after all, when your ego is humiliated, it feels pretty close to death. It's easy to get humility and self-judgment confused! Humility is not condemnation but a beautiful form of self-love. It's where respect for God's way and radical honesty about reality meet. It's the ability to hold loosely your sense of what you deserve while holding tightly to the way you can show up for others. In some ways, it's about losing yourself, but only losing the stuff—pride, resentment, and the right to be offended (not to mention the right to be right)—that's best to burn anyway. Humility is about displacing yourself as the most important thing in the universe and seeing yourself instead as one small being with an important role to play in a big, beautiful, mysterious world.

> Humility is where respect for God's way and radical honesty about reality meet.

When Joseph resisted Potiphar's wife, she was humiliated and did what prideful people do—she shifted blame and covered for herself. She accused and then framed Joseph, first in front of the servants and then to her husband. Once again, Joseph found himself a captive, this time in a literal prison. But as in the first chapter of his unexpected season, when Joseph moved from the pit into captivity in Potiphar's house: "The LORD was with him; he showed him kindness and granted him favor in the eyes of the prison warden" (Genesis 39:21). Just in case we missed it the first time around, we see God extending blessing *through* Joseph. God's kindness did not lead him to take Joseph out of prison or even give him an extra meal or a private room. God's kindness allowed Joseph to be a blessing to others. And Joseph's response was continued faithfulness to whatever was right in front of him.

Humility is a choice. It's allowing God to be the author and director of your story, even if that story is unfolding in the hospital room you hate or the workplace you dread or the pit or prison of your life—whatever that pit or prison looks like for you. Humility is seeing each day as an opportunity to gain knowledge, for "with the humble is wisdom."[1] Humility led Joseph to continue showing up to serve, to go above and beyond with anything he was given to do. It wasn't long before the warden gave Joseph more responsibility. Like Potiphar, the warden came to trust Joseph, until he "paid no attention to anything under Joseph's care" (Genesis 39:23). Time passed. Joseph kept showing up. God kept granting him favor. And as Joseph kept passing the test of integrity, he also passed the test of humility.

You might be thinking, *Well, he didn't have much choice in the matter, did he? . . . Sold into slavery and thrown into prison isn't exactly the land of the free.* But Joseph *did* have to make choices in prison, and even if you are experiencing the limits of your season—perhaps even with all your rights and opportunities stripped away—you still have choices to make. You alone determine your attitude, your outlook, your hope.

Eyes on Others

Joseph had that choice—and he chose wisely. When the king's cupbearer and baker offended their ruler, he threw them in prison—the same prison where Joseph was kept. Joseph was assigned to take care of them. And he showed up for these two men in the same way he'd shown up for Potiphar and the warden. He didn't just do the minimum or dial it in. He noticed. He cared. And he engaged with them.

I appreciate the following perspective on humility from Nipun Mehta, the founder of a service organization focused on creating a movement of good through small acts of kindness.

> Without humility, our overblown sense of entitlement disconnects us. It increases narcissism and reduces empathy. That may be good for the economy but certainly not for

societal well-being. A couple of months ago I was in Bhutan with the folks who implemented Gross National Happiness, and from them I learned about some remarkable research at the University of Michigan. It turns out that ever since 1980, our empathy levels have been gradually dropping, but in 2000, they suddenly plummeted 40 percent. Forty! Not surprisingly, a Gallup report just released last week reported that the US has dropped from 12th position to number 23 on the global well-being index. It's a strange paradox, we are at the same time, more self-centered than ever, and less happy and healthy for it.[2]

We can opine about why our empathy levels are dropping and our anxiety and depression are skyrocketing. We can also consider, as Mehta illuminates here, the connection between our loss of empathy and our loss of happiness. Interestingly, according to a more recent World Happiness Report, the happiness of US citizens noticeably increased a few years ago, and researchers attribute that to an increase in helping strangers, making donations, and volunteering—actions of empathy and humility—during the COVID-19 pandemic.[3]

Mehta suggests that it's only in moving toward humility that we can elevate the "specialness of others"—which has the greatest impact on the world around us. "Happiness loves company," he says. "Everything we do ripples out and affects each strand in the web of our connections."[4] It's when we decenter ourselves that we create the most impact on the world—and experience the most satisfaction ourselves.

For proof, we need look no further than Joseph's approach to his next season—humiliated by Potiphar's wife, stripped again of his identity, and back in a pit—to understand the power and purpose of humility. But make no mistake: Humility is a virtue that stands in complete opposition to the human desire to acquire and achieve, to center ourselves as important and admirable. Humility gives us the ability to place ourselves into a position to serve.

One night Pharaoh's cupbearer and baker each had strange and detailed dreams. When Joseph saw them the next morning, "he noticed that they both looked upset" (Genesis 40:6, NLT). He paid attention. He was not too caught up in his own story, in his own uncertainty, in his own pain to notice. He took note of their pain, and then he engaged with them. And it's *only* because he acknowledged that pain that his opportunity for redemption began.

"Why do you look so sad today?" Joseph asked (Genesis 40:7), and he discovered that they had no one to interpret their troublesome dreams. His humility led him to notice their need, and his humility guided his response: "Do not interpretations belong to God? Tell me your dreams" (Genesis 40:8). Humility is a mix of presence and confidence. It's being able to trust God despite not knowing why you are in this season while still believing He's planning to use you in the very place of your suffering, discomfort, or pain. When we stay fixated on our own pain, when we spend our energy blaming ourselves or others for our situation, we are self-oriented. We are simply unable to notice and respond to the needs around us. That's the deception of pride, the great and devious pattern of orienting the world with ourselves at the center. Humility is the choice to decenter your pain as the primary driver of your choices and to recenter your purpose on trusting God's timing, planning, and presence in even the most painful of seasons.

Humility makes us willing to help, but it also enables us to ask for help. Because after Joseph interpreted the dreams of both the cupbearer and the baker, he called on their assistance:

> *When all goes well with you, remember me and show me kindness; mention me to Pharaoh and get me out of this prison. I was forcibly carried off from the land of the Hebrews, and even here I have done nothing to deserve being put in a dungeon.*
> GENESIS 40:14-15

Notice that humility is not about skipping and stuffing, pretending it's not really that bad. It's not about dwelling and diving, creating a spiritual myopia that keeps you focused only on your own pain. Humility leads you to be real and redeemed, to be helpful and admit that you need help. It enables you to see small and ordinary opportunities to serve as sacred offerings in the midst of your uncertainty. It enables you to see yourself rightly.

As Mother Teresa said, "If you are humble nothing will touch you, neither praise nor disgrace, because you know what you are."[5]

Blessings and Dreams, in Jesus' Name

Humility also reorients our vision of what leads to a rewarding and meaningful life. We are steeped in a culture that (often unknowingly to us) shapes our dreams and defines the good life very differently from the way God intended. Most of us develop a me-centered mindset because we want to "get ahead" and be happy. But what if there's a better dream to carry, one that can sustain us through even the worst of times?

Here's the promise embedded in this great test, the test of humility: *Humility allows even the worst season to be used for the best dream.* The test of humility is the invitation to joy. To receive joy is to receive gifts from God that allow you to prosper even in your worst pain. To receive joy is to believe that God still has intentions for you today, that God can bless you abundantly with His comfort and presence in a way that allows you to live joyfully for others— yes, right in the midst of your pain. But in order to do that, you have to let go of what was, and replace it with a new dream.

So let's fast-forward past Genesis to the Gospels for a moment so we can look at how Jesus realigns our dreams—and models the humility that allows us to accept them. Before we get to the dream itself, let's consider how radical Jesus' teaching truly was—so radical that even His closest friends didn't get it. What Jesus invited His followers into was a new kingdom—a place we experience right now, a new way of living in every sense of the word. Like us, Jesus' disciples were often confused about how one "showed" they were serious about Jesus and His kingdom teaching. They wanted to figure out what it meant to be in or out, and they definitely wanted to stay close to Jesus and His power. They argued among themselves about who was the greatest. They rebuked other people when they cast out demons in Jesus' name, probably annoyed to find out that accessing Jesus' power was an equal-opportunity experience, whether or not someone was one of the Twelve.[6] At one point, the disciples James and John had their mom ask Jesus to give them the right and left seat in His kingdom (Matthew 20:21). When Jesus warned the disciples of His approaching arrest and crucifixion, Peter boasted, "Even if I have to die with you, I will never disown you" (Matthew 26:35). They wanted to rank themselves and prove to Jesus that they deserved to be "in." But they would learn that coming into the kingdom of God has nothing to do with who deserves it—it has everything to do with the One who dreamed it up in the first place.

When Jesus came preaching the Good News of the kingdom of God, He wasn't interested in becoming a self-help guru who would assist people in fulfilling their own dreams. He wasn't talking just about how to get to heaven (although eternity is part of the message). He wasn't just modeling a sinner's prayer (although Jesus teaches us to pray). Jesus came to proclaim that, with His arrival, the kingdom of heaven was now among us. The blessing once reserved for God's chosen people, Israel, had now been extended to "everyone who calls on the name of the Lord" (Romans 10:13). In other words, the God of Abraham, Isaac, and Jacob—men who had experienced the faithfulness of God despite their failures and who had passed on their stories to Joseph—was now inviting us into their story through Jesus Christ.

What's more, Jesus clarified what it means to be blessed and gave us a dream of what it means to live out the kingdom of heaven in the here and now. Jesus' most famous message, recorded in Matthew 5 through 7 and more succinctly in Luke 6, turns everything we know about blessing on its head. Jesus declared that the blessed are those who are "poor in spirit" and "those who mourn."[7] We're blessed, He said, when people hate us, exclude us, insult us, and reject us. Pastor and author Tim Keller says, "The things the world puts at the bottom of its list are at the top of the kingdom of God's list."[8] But why in the world would you want to be a part of a kingdom where all of these things make someone "blessed"? Unless, of course, we have been wrong about what makes a good life. Unless there's something so distinctly important about our unexpected seasons because of where they lead.

After shocking us with a new definition of blessing (apparently not found in luxury goods, first-class accommodations, or the perfect marriage, much to everyone's chagrin), Jesus clarified what makes true disciples. Once again, it's much different from the image we humans came up with. So what dream does Jesus offer? It is not about the circumstances of your life. This dream is rooted in a much deeper truth, one that outlasts positions, titles, relationships, and seasons of life. Your job, your marriage, your friendships, your health are all a part of this dream, but they are not the dream itself. The dream is evergreen, accessible to everyone, but it's only experienced by those who take the middle way, the real and redeemed way. It's a dream that may take everything from you but give you back unexpected abundance in return. Through His life, Jesus offers a dream that looks like this:

a life of freedom (Luke 4:18)
a mind governed by life and peace (Romans 8:6)
love we can never be separated from (Romans 8:35)
a calling and purpose (Ephesians 4:1)
strength and power through the Spirit (Ephesians 6:10)

And this is just a small sampling. The dream is real, and it's yours through Christ. But to glory with Christ is also to glory in suffering (1 Peter 4:13), which means we'll continue to face the test of humility—and we must respond to it.

Here's the Problem Though ...

Humility sounds good on paper but is much harder to practice. Perhaps like me, you vacillate between wanting someone to notice and care about how you are doing, and wanting to disappear and not be noticed at all. The truth is, there's a small, grasping side to all of us. We worry that if we quietly keep serving and giving, no one will remember us or care about our needs, desires, and dreams. There's a reason for the idiom that "the squeaky wheel gets the grease." It feels like the only way to get ahead is to get loud, get noticed, and get yourself in the very center of the action.

That greedy, grasping self in each of us is never satisfied. Sometimes the self rises up in protest because we don't get what we want—the dream is deferred. And sometimes the self rises up to protest that what we thought we wanted is not actually enough. As it turns out, the problem isn't about what we have or don't have. The problem is that very self, the part of us that wants to be exalted and elevated.

Or perhaps like Joseph, it's not a lack of humility that's hurt you—you've experienced direct suffering *because* of your humility. You were willing to serve and to give and to love, and now it's backfired in your face. The promises of God feel like they've turned to ash. But whether you are struggling to be humble or are sad about where your humility put you, the way forward is the same: The way of Jesus is the only path to the peace and joy of the kingdom.

The way of Jesus is unequivocally humble. He is drawn to the humble. He loves kids. He loves people who admit their need. He loves and notices those who serve generously. He loves and notices those who give. He even loves to tells stories about ordinary stuff like bread, seeds, and annoying friends.

Jesus modeled humility from beginning to end. And at what seemed to be the most bitter finish in the most unexpected season, Jesus was hung on a cross, lifted up in an excruciating act of terror, flanked on each side by convicted criminals. Think of the humblest thing a person can experience:

doing good but being unjustly condemned for doing wrong;
loving fully but being betrayed;
giving sacrificially but then being abandoned;
teaching a lifestyle of serving and being accused of power grabbing.

Imagine experiencing all of that—and still loving. Still giving. Still forgiving. This is the story of Jesus, hung on that cross between thieves. In contrast to one another, the men on either side of Jesus embody opposing attitudes: pride and humility. The first condemned man sneered at Jesus and said (my paraphrase), "If You are so great, why don't You save Yourself and us too?" (see Luke 23:39). The perfect picture of pride is both his arrogant insult to God incarnate and his audacity to believe that he deserved to be saved despite his crime.

But the man on the other side of Jesus rebuked the first. "We are getting what our deeds deserve," he said (Luke 23:41). He was a picture of humility. But humility isn't just acceptance, it's also hope. The humble criminal named reality, but he followed it with a hopeful request. Through his own painful, gasping breaths, he requested of Jesus, "Remember me when you come into your kingdom" (verse 42). And Jesus, in His own pain, far worse because He was bearing both physical suffering and the spiritual weight of the world's sin, responded with love. He answered humility with his own humility: "Today you will be with me in paradise" (verse 43). Even minutes from death, Jesus extended life.

Through His life, teaching, and sacrificial death, Jesus clarified the endgame for us. Through His example, we learn this truth: It is actually a blessing to be helpless, to mourn, to be passed over, and to live in the uncertainty of everything falling apart because that is where we discover the deeper joy and lasting hope of the presence of Christ.

The Dream Is (Actually) Alive

So how did this kingdom life ultimately impact Jesus' disciples? They may have been clueless through much of Jesus' earthly ministry, but Peter and the other disciples wised up when confronted with the risen Christ and empowered by the Holy Spirit. Acts 2 records the first public message given after Jesus' death and resurrection that proclaimed who Jesus was, what He did, and why it mattered for everyone. The preacher is Peter. Let's review Peter's experience before we hear his sermon. Peter is the disciple who'd boastfully insisted just a few weeks before that nothing would ever come between him and his leader, Jesus. (Remember his words in Matthew 26:35: "I will never disown you.") Yet immediately following Jesus' arrest, Peter denied knowing Jesus multiple times (with a curse!). When it was time to put his words into action, Peter failed.

Peter is like us. We often believe we can do more and be more than we actually can. Peter had a moment of humiliation that we might all experience as a deal-breaker. The dream is not for a guy who claims to be Jesus' number one follower, only to deny and abandon Jesus at His greatest hour of need. But praise be to God, His kingdom is one of kindness and grace offered to us even as we realize how much we don't deserve it. This happened for Peter when the resurrected Christ extended relationship to Peter again (John 21:15-19). Even at his worst, Peter was still loved and accepted. Likewise, even when we fall apart because of our own doing or what's been done to us, Jesus is still present, still offering the choice to experience the joyful kingdom of God through Him.

This Peter—the one who failed, the one who was humbled—was now the person preaching the first recorded post-Resurrection sermon. A few weeks after his "not what I signed up for" experience, Peter announced with passion, conviction, and courage what following Christ is truly about. In his sermon, he quoted the Old Testament prophet Joel who said that in the end, when the Messiah (Jesus) is near, "your old men will dream dreams" (Acts 2:17). In other words, the long-held dream of the Israelites that the kingdom of God would come, that the Messiah would reign—that dream is fulfilled now through Christ. What's more, that dream is not limited to the Israelites—Joseph's people—it's a dream for all of us. The kingdom is established; that time is *now*. We are living in that dream.

When the crowd asked what they should do in response to this truth, Peter replied, "Repent and be baptized. . . . And you will receive the gift of the Holy Spirit" (Acts 2:38). The instruction then is the same now. When we come to Jesus, we admit our own lack, our inability to do life on our own, and our great desire to have our needs met in Him. In other words, we repent. We turn away from our own kingdom and embrace Jesus as our king. We declare publicly that we are followers of Jesus. And we receive the gift of the Holy Spirit—the person of God who actually dwells with us, who guides us into truth, who comforts us, who gives us direction, who gives us power. We are no longer alone. We have God's presence, and we also have God's purpose. Through the Holy Spirit, we have the power to live into the dream God has for our lives: "You will receive power when the Holy Spirit comes on you; and you will be my witnesses in Jerusalem, and in all Judea and Samaria, and to the ends of the earth" (Acts 1:8).

Your be-all and end-all, the place where blessing is experienced in you and through you, is in the way you bear witness to

Jesus. To bear witness is to simply report your experience with Jesus. Much like the kingdom of heaven itself, this experience cannot be reduced to doctrine, behavior, church attendance, or civic engagement alone, although these are all impacted by your experience of Jesus. It's not signified by how much less you swear or how much money you give to charity or how you treat the homeless guy on the corner, although all of that will also be impacted by Jesus.

Living out the dream is about living out your story with Christ, especially when the story takes a turn into what you never would have signed up for. And at the crossroads, where you realize this season you are in is difficult, uncertain, and has no easy resolution—the decision between walking with Jesus or walking alone comes down to this one thing: humility.

Acceptance is the first test of humility. Acceptance says, "This is not what I want, but God is still in it with me." Acceptance says, "I would not choose this, but I am not God, so I'll let Him choose." Acceptance is not denial. Acceptance does not mean you don't mourn (remember that leads to a blessing!). Acceptance doesn't mean you can't question or wrestle or even flat-out fight with God about what's happening, but it also means that when you move away from God, you don't stay there. You come back to Him. Only humility allows you to stay in the present of your unexpected season. Only humility says, "I am in pain about the past and anxious about the future, but I choose to stay in the present to find out what God has for me right now."

Acceptance is the first test of humility.

Humility allows us to keep believing the dream. It allows us to see that no matter the circumstance, we continue to live out our story in the kingdom of God. Unexpected seasons force us to look inward and ask: *Who am I?* and *Who am I becoming?* But humility allows us to surrender: *God is God, and I am not*, and to focus our attention outward: *Blessing is not about what's happening to me but through me.*

Humble or Be Humbled

Humility will come to us all. Anyone who has stood at the bedside of someone who is dying understands deep in their core that we will all be humbled eventually. But there are two paths to humility. The first is to humble yourself. It's the decision to wake up to your reality, to say to God, "I don't know why this is the way it is, and I don't know when it will end, but I trust You. I want to serve You. I will humble myself to show up today with joy and obedience and a heart to serve others." In this way, Joseph's servant attitude foreshadowed the perfect humility of Jesus.

The other way is to be humbled. I don't know about you, but even my worst day with God is better than an hour against God. Living against God is rejecting Him and living in pride. And God will ultimately oppose the proud (James 4:6). God will stand up to whatever is proud in us, and sometimes He will use our struggles to humble us. This is why even our worst season can bring us the greatest gains. The pain that makes us desperate can also make us real. It may make us weak, but it can also make us whole.

I've often struggled to understand how all the bad can actually bring good in the kingdom of God. Why would a good God want me to suffer, to feel pain, to be excluded by others? Maybe you, too, have wondered why a good God would allow [fill in the blank] to happen. And that's not a question I would be so arrogant to believe I could answer for you here. But what I do know, what you've told me in your stories, and what I've experienced for myself in quiet moments after a sermon or between retreat sessions or in the grocery store parking lot is that maybe the real blessing isn't about the suffering or pain; it's about the humility these trials create in our spirits. Maybe it's about getting in touch with our helplessness, which makes us aware of God's presence and love. Maybe it's when we feel totally emptied that we can be filled with God rather than with all the things and circumstances that masquerade as blessings in our lives.

Then we, like Jesus, can introduce others to our loving Father: "Keep open house; be generous with your lives. By opening up to others, you'll prompt people to open up with God, this generous Father in heaven" (Matthew 5:16, MSG).

This is the blessing. This is the dream. This is the humble, gentle approach of the kingdom of heaven, the one you are invited to embrace—even (and especially) when it's not going the way you want; even (and especially) in the waiting. Even in the uncertainty, even when it feels like all is lost, you still control your attitude. And the dream is still yours to give.

After Joseph noticed that the king's servants were dejected, after he interpreted the cupbearer's and baker's dreams correctly, after he asked the cupbearer to remember him and speak to the king on his behalf—this is the moment when we wait for the story to turn, when we expect things to get better. Surely after all of this waiting and obeying, God will reward Joseph and come through! Surely Joseph will be vindicated and elevated. Doesn't that feel like God's favor?

So Joseph interpreted the dreams. He relayed both interpretations with courage and integrity. The cupbearer would be restored to his position. The baker would be executed. On their way out, Joseph said to the cupbearer, *Remember me.*

And yet.

Yet [even after all that] the chief cupbearer did not remember Joseph, but forgot [all about] him.[9]
GENESIS 40:23, AMP

So what happens after the tests? We enter into trust.

A PRAYER OF SURRENDER

God,

*I cast my cares upon You
because You care for me.*

Jesus,

*I choose to accept
Your peace as my peace.
I choose to make every effort
toward peace today.*

*In the power of the Spirit,
I choose thankfulness over discouragement,
hope over despair,
trust over defeat.*

*In Your power and in Your name,
Amen.*

PART 2

TRUSTING

*Never be afraid to trust an unknown future
to a known God.*

CORRIE TEN BOOM

Yet [even after all that] the chief cupbearer did not remember Joseph, but forgot [all about] him.

GENESIS 40:23, AMP

CHAPTER 6

TRUST HIM: KNOWING AND EXPERIENCING GOD

He who trusts in himself is lost. He who
trusts in God can do all things.

ST. ALPHONSUS LIGUORI

After enduring the tests of loss, integrity, and humility, we enter into another season—not one any of us want. This is the interlude, the time between testing and triumph. This is when we learn if our trust can bear the weight of our pain. This is when we learn what—and who—we can actually trust. And all of this happens in the waiting—the place where our trust is deepened.

Sometimes this period of waiting is chosen for us, and sometimes we ourselves are so paralyzed or uncertain that we are frozen in indecision. After I left my position at church, I thought I'd spend a few months resting and resetting and then things would sort themselves out. I didn't know what was next, but I thought I trusted God enough to ride it out. Then we entered the pandemic. And the things I thought would sort themselves out just . . . didn't.

> The interlude is the time between testing and triumph.

Conversations that I thought I'd have, opportunities that surely would appear, relationships that would endure—one by one, my circumstances just didn't sort out. I had trusted in so many things to be the source of my strength and my worth, and not one of them remained as it had been before. Then right in the middle of that season, I was skiing with my youngest son and injured my knee, which required surgery and intensive rehab. I had enjoyed being strong and athletic all my life, and now even my body wasn't sorting out anymore. What strikes me as I retell this story is how interminably long it all felt. It wasn't an all-of-a-sudden crisis; it was the slow death of many things and many dreams. Yet it was also in those deaths that space was being cleared in my soul for new things. But at the time, it all felt barren.

And Joseph Waits

For Joseph, that interlude happens as we bridge Genesis 40 and 41. It's the gap—in his case, the waiting that came after he interpreted the cupbearer's dream. Let's review: Joseph, the favorite son of Jacob, was cast into a pit and sold into slavery at seventeen. He was sold in Egypt, where he worked for a chief government official, Potiphar, before once again being cast into a "pit," the king's prison. After eleven long years of praying, showing up for Potiphar in his house, and then being faithful in prison, Joseph had the chance to interpret the dreams of two of the king's men. Afterward, he asked for one of the men's help, and we feel the story beginning to turn.

Finally.

Finally!

Finally, Joseph's dark season would end, finally Joseph would be vindicated, finally God would make good on His promises, right? Eleven years is a long time to wait for anything, especially when you've been wronged! The cupbearer was released from prison and reinstated at the palace, where . . .

He forgot all about Joseph.

And two more years passed.

After what must have already been long years of slavery and prison, just when it seemed hope had arrived and his fortune was changing . . . nothing. Nothing happened. Joseph properly gave God credit for his ability to decipher dreams before correctly interpreting the cupbearer's dream. (He also accurately interpreted the baker's dream, which ended in that man's death. A stark reminder that obedience isn't always easy.) So Joseph asked the one living servant to remember him. And I imagine that Joseph's faith in God, along with the chance to make that direct and courageous appeal, created a level of hope in Joseph that he hadn't known in quite some time.

I picture Joseph waking up in the dungeon with a spark in his heart for those first few days after the cupbearer's vindication. *Maybe today is the day.* I imagine what it must have been like to feel that ember smoldering day after day, and no help coming. At some point, the fire went out. The spark was extinguished. The dream died—again.

When we face our own setbacks, when we have hope that things are turning around and then they do an about-face and get even worse, our natural tendency is to retrace our steps and figure out where we went wrong. *Was I too much for this person, or too little? Should I have tried harder, or given up sooner? Why didn't I read the signs of where this was all going?* The crowd around us—our social media feeds, celebrities, TV shows—encourages us to do this too. It's so tempting to try to identify the reason for every problem because knowing the cause feels like control. If we can explain a thing, we can contain a thing. This line of thinking illuminates our cultural narrative of the individualistic meritocracy, the faulty belief that we'll be rewarded if we just try hard enough and are good enough.

What do we do when God's promises seem far away and grief feels ever present? When it feels like somewhere along the way, we must have fallen out of God's favor or, even worse, from His awareness altogether?

The idea that God would delay justice and allow His faithful servants to continue suffering doesn't feel right, and I don't think it's something we want to believe. But that's where we go wrong: So often our unexpected seasons, which come to all of us at some point, don't resolve quickly. And it's the slowness of things changing, healing, growing, and shifting that provides us with an incredible opportunity to dismantle any false notions we have of who God is and how He works so we can reconstruct our beliefs into something stronger, more resilient, and more true.

We do that in three ways:

First, we have to trust God. We have to know what we can know and then allow experiences to fill the gaps in our knowledge. We'll talk about that in this chapter.

Second, we have to trust the opportunities. We'll discover what that kind of trust looks like in action in chapter 7.

Finally, we must learn to trust our tears—to understand that both lament and grief are channels that bring us into deeper places with God where our souls can truly be nourished. That's chapter 8.

We never know how long the season will last, so our trust can't come from knowing the timeline. Our trust can come only from knowing the One who sets time in the first place.

The Issue of God's Timing

I've had a long and contentious relationship with God's timing. After racing through high school like my pants were on fire, I graduated college at the wise age of nineteen, ready to "launch into life"—and promptly discovered that life doesn't work on my timeline. I was laid off from my first corporate bank job before I even started. Then I took a job selling two-year fitness memberships to overly optimistic women at an all-ladies gym. It took nearly a year of furious and anxious job seeking to land a new corporate position—very entry level and with a much smaller salary than the one at the bank but a big step-up from the gym. When I felt ready to switch roles at that company, I was told I wasn't eligible because not enough time had passed. (I then quit.)

By then I was married and pregnant. Our first child was ten days overdue. It took me twice as long to finish grad school as I'd expected because of said baby. I felt ready to lead before I did, ready to publish before I did, ready to preach before I did, ready to move when it wasn't quite time. When my kids were little, I was ready for them to be bigger. When they got bigger, I was ready for them to drive. When they drove, I wanted all of it to rewind. I am constantly out of sync. God seems to have set my brain on 1.5x speed, and it's caused nothing but trouble.

Yet as much as I hate to admit it, waiting is a fierce but fruitful teacher. In the rocky ground between what I hoped for and what I experienced is an opportunity for something entirely new to grow. I do not welcome this rocky ground, and frankly, I don't think I'm very good at cultivating it. But it seems as if some lessons can only be learned here. This place teaches us what it means to trust God without any immediate evidence for why we should continue to put our faith in Him. This rocky place reveals what our faith is really built upon. It uncovers our doubts; unearths our shame, anger, and insecurity; and often reveals our shocking inability to apply our knowledge of God's goodness to our reality—be it the prison or the palace.

This interlude forces us to engage with our doubts about whether God is actually in control and what our role is during the waiting. In our binary belief system, God being in control of everything and me having a part to play in it just doesn't add up. After all, if God is fully in control, why can't I just stay in bed and let the world pass me by until He says "go" again? But if God is not fully in control, does that mean I'm the one who caused all this mess, and I'm paying for it now? If we stare that problem of power in its ugly face and the waiting still drags on, we might even get to the most courageous question of all: *If God is so good, why did He allow this to happen?*

Trust isn't something you set and forget. Trust isn't something you learn and master. Trust is an active, rigorous, intentional decision to live according to something you cannot always see. Trust is taking the shimmers and glimmers of God's presence and love and creating a mosaic of meaning that you can call beautiful. It's letting God be your source of life one day at a time, praying just for your daily bread, no more. It's discovering that there are still good things to be found even in those barren seasons.

But here's a hard truth that I've learned in my own "not what I signed up for" season: *Trust can't be trust until it's tested over time.*

My own experience with trusting God is rigorous. It's uneven. It takes work. Every day I'm learning to trust Him, and even after almost thirty years of solid Jesus following, anything in my life that feels undone or unredeemed seems to mock me, suggesting that God isn't steadfast in the way I think He is. After all, God might be trustworthy in the sense that He's holy, that He's in charge. That's one way to see it. But when the anxiety lies heavy on your chest at night, when you cry in the shower, when you desperately long for God to give you something—anything—to keep you going when all you feel is darkness, distance, and silence, it can be hard to believe that He is everything He says He is—not just powerful and in control but good, loving, and merciful. The true task in these seasons is to believe that in the deepest parts of our pain, God is still trustworthy in all these ways.

He is powerful. He is in control. He is good.

Think about that. Those three constants often stand in tension with one another: Powerful. In Control. Good. Which words can you fully claim to be true about God based on your own relationship with Him? Where has your unexpected season created doubt, tension, or anger?

To answer those questions, I have to take a minute to get in touch with the honest place in myself. I have to dig deep and pull out some painful and undone memories. When I do, I realize that I can trust that God is powerful and in control—I've seen enough to know that's true. But what causes tension for me is His goodness. It's so hard to admit and even harder to write, but as I examine my own story with its painful places, I want to ask, as a child to her father, "But how could this be good?"

As much as I hate it, I begrudgingly acknowledge that it's only as I'm waiting that I enter fully into the deeper questions of trust. Testing gives us a quick feedback loop, but trusting is what grows from testing over time.

I've wanted to hurry through the hard seasons. I've wanted to process faster, grieve more quickly, heal rapidly.

> Truth grounded in experience is what creates unshakable trust.

But the thing about healing is that there's no such thing as speeding it up. You heal when you heal. You grow when you grow. And as you heal, you grow, gaining a deeper understanding of what you know and what you should do with that knowledge. This knowing occurs when what you think and feel come together—it's truth with experience. Truth grounded in experience is what creates unshakable trust.

Knowing What We Can Know

When it comes to trusting God, problems arise when we aren't exactly sure what—or who—we are trusting. Our minds try to fill in the gaps of what we don't know, often in ways outside of our awareness. We believe in the goodness of God because our kids don't get cancer. We believe in the mercy of God because we didn't have that near-tragic car accident. We believe in the power of God because we have an emotional response to a beautiful song or word. In the ordinary times of life, this knowledge is enough. But unfortunately, this knowledge is neither deep enough nor true enough for the unexpected seasons, when we do get the diagnosis, we do have the accident, and we feel wooden or numb no matter how inspiring the music. When our circumstances fail us, we are exposed to the limits of our knowledge. And we may find that our assumptions take us to places of confusion and doubt. One anonymous reader wrote in, "Why am I going through this challenge despite the fact that I'm starting a new and healthy chapter in my life?" Another said, "When they've averted something bad, why do so many people say that God was good to them? Does that mean He wasn't good to me?"

These questions feel powerful because they are. Puzzles like these always lead us to one place: Who is God really, and can I trust Him? This is a question we ask individually in the unexpected, and a question we are asking collectively in our post-COVID-19 world. Recent studies report that belief in God and church attendance are down, particularly among young people—although the vast majority of Americans still say they believe in God.[1]

Interestingly, there's plenty of evidence that faith enriches our lives. One robust study done over a century indicates that strong belief, weekly church attendance, and close-knit friendships create lives with less anxiety, less depression, and more personal satisfaction overall. It's incredibly good for us to not only believe in God but also order life around that belief. In terms of being very satisfied with life, weekly church attendance creates a stronger sense of satisfaction than making $100,000 or more a year.[2] Even the mighty dollar can't compete with a belief in God.

So we have a tension to address—we want to believe in God, and we have the nod in popular culture to the reality that this strong action-oriented belief in God is actually good for us too. But as any thoughtful person would, we also have big questions about God that suggest that what we might be struggling with most is knowledge: Who does God say He is and what does He say He can do?

In 2022, Gallup reported that "42 percent of all Americans . . . say God hears prayers and can intervene on a person's behalf.

Meanwhile, 28 percent . . . say God hears prayers but cannot intervene, while 11 percent think God does neither." Another 17 percent said they don't believe in God at all.[3] In other words, less than half of US adults think God is both personal and powerful in individual lives.

So maybe believing in God isn't the difficulty; instead, it's wondering who this God is anyway. Many of us, when we face this kind of question, freak out and avoid. We've tried to be good and humble, and now we are just tired. We don't want to face the big questions about God, so we bypass the questions by escaping from or numbing the pain. We find comfort in cookies or Pinterest or spreadsheets or ESPN or alcohol. We scroll, shop, or gamble online. We obsessively try insignificant fixes to grab some kind of control. The questions feel too big and too hard to answer. Knowing God feels like trying to hold smoke or water you've scooped in your hands: Impossible to grasp with nothing to show for the effort.

I developed a strange fascination with our spice drawer during this season of loss in my own life. Something about using a little funnel to transfer all my spices from disorganized, mismatched jars into perfectly coordinated bottles with minimalist labels in a beautiful font was both comforting and distracting. I couldn't fix the trajectory of my work, the nagging worries I had about my children, my dull and hurried quiet time. But I could funnel spices from perfectly good jars into other perfectly good (but prettier) jars and, boy, that felt good.

But at some point, the spice jars are organized, the scrolling gets old, and we look up from our glazed-over dissociation to a life that we still have to live. We can endeavor to escape, but we can never escape ourselves. Our stories, experiences, and pain will stay with us, no matter how far we stuff them away. And the courageous journey in the "not what I signed up for" season begins when we decide to reckon with these big questions. Trusting God without asking the questions will eventually stop working. Before we can trust God with unexpected seasons and our stories, our futures, and our very selves, we have to know God for who He says He is.

Knowing God: Opening Our Eyes to His Goodness

The first thing God wants us to know about Him is His goodness. Another way to say it might be His "merciful generosity alongside moral excellence." One evidence of this quality is seen in common grace—the idea that God showers His goodness on both the righteous and the wicked, that God restrains evil in this world, and that God can use even those who are morally corrupt to accomplish good things.

That's a deep concept, so let's frame it another way. The Bible tells us that God "sends rain on the just and on the unjust" (Matthew 5:45, ESV). Rain sustains creation, which sustains us. Regardless of our status, God continues to bestow provision and beauty on our world. Hebrews 1:2-3 adds that Jesus sustains all things through His Word and that through Christ, God "also . . . made the universe." *The universe.* So often we think of Jesus as our personal God, and He is, no doubt, personal. But if we think of Jesus only as our personal God, we miss out on the magnitude and power of His glory. It should be mind-blowing to realize that Jesus, the One who came to serve and show what the kingdom is all about, holds up the universe by the word of His goodness. Think about it: The goodness of the One who loved kids, fishermen, prostitutes, soldiers, and scholars, who put up with people's questions, criticisms, complete lack of interest and curiosity to even try to *get it*—that goodness never fails or runs out. It continues to provide, sustain, and bring beauty to everyone—good and evil, just and unjust.

When you are in a season in which nothing in your story seems good, focusing on the goodness you experience as His common grace can be your lifeline from one day to the next. Yesterday I took a walk around our block, counting up everything I could experience as God's common grace: the warmth of the sun on my face, the marvel of a leaf just beginning to tinge red as the summer turned toward fall, my dog's tail wagging when he came across a water bowl set out in front of the little shop down the street. Maybe that water bowl is the common grace version for dogs—a moment of refreshment, created by someone else, just for the sheer enjoyment of caring for creatures. Maybe we all need water bowls in our stories, the moments of goodness that come even when life feels like it's crashing around us.

Common grace is also about the goodness of God to restrain evil. In Romans 13:1, the apostle Paul says God is the One behind civil jurisdiction, systems of government, rulers, and authorities. A quirky story in Genesis shows that God can also restrain the evil acts of humans—whether saints like Abraham or sinners like a Philistine king (Genesis 20:6). When I think about the wars and rumors of wars that I've experienced just in my lifetime, I might expect that the planet would have been obliterated a few times over by now. God's goodness is upholding and sustaining our world. (Now let me pause and say that if you're in the midst of an unexpected season, it's hard to read that without immediately being triggered to ask, *If God is so good then why did He allow _____ to happen to me?* That is an important and sacred question that we will spend time on soon, so I invite you to hold the tension of your personal experience while we consider some universal truths about the nature of God.)

Finally, common grace is about the moral compass God has placed in everyone. This is the human instinct toward right and wrong. For if there were no God, or not a good God, why would people even cooperate at all? Why would we wrestle and struggle to create beauty, harmony, and peace if our only instinct were survival of the fittest? Romans 2 reasons that if human beings who are far from God still follow a moral code (for instance, almost everyone reviles people who commit sexual crimes against children), then that moral compass is evidence of God's existence. Moral relativism, apparently, is not always relative.

So why is this important for you right now? Because for each of us individually, nothing calls into question the goodness of God more than our own disappointment, confusion, and grief about the way things are. We cannot always claim that we are *experiencing* God as good if we are relying only on our short-term memory. But we can *know* God is good when we lift our gaze above our circumstances long enough to seek His goodness outside our pain, in the common graces of His nature and redemptive stories.

Knowing God: Acknowledging His Power

I have never encountered a storm so fierce and so fast as the one I drove into one summer evening in Arkansas. My compact rental car shuddered down the highway as gusts of wind buffeted the right side of the vehicle so forcefully that I had to counteract them by steering into the wind. Branches and debris were flying horizontally across the highway, and the combination of rain, wind, and light blurred the horizon as if I had pulled a gray sweatshirt over my face. I squinted my eyes as I drove slowly forward, praying for an overpass or some kind of shelter to appear. The hazard lights of a truck in front of me were my only beacon. Eventually I found the overpass and the storm blew away, but the memory remains, a perfect picture of how easy it is to forget that God is powerful—until you see real power. "The hand of the LORD is powerful."[4]

There's a scene in the movie *Forrest Gump* in which Forrest's troubled platoon leader, Lieutenant Dan, finally has it out with God. Lieutenant Dan had lost his legs in an enemy attack during the Vietnam War and spent the next several years trying to forget. He was killing himself slowly, the life leaking out of him from drugs, alcohol, and anger. Sometimes he directed that anger toward Forrest, who had saved his superior from death but forced him to deal with his disabled condition.

Years later, Lieutenant Dan found himself back with Forrest, working on a shrimping boat together (and failing miserably). But one night while standing at the top of the boat's mast in the middle of a hurricane, Lieutenant Dan railed at God. He shook his fists, screaming, "You call this a storm!" He finally went face-to-face with his own demons—using the power of the storm to challenge the power of a God who calls life good, even in the worst seasons. The next morning, the sky had cleared and Lieutenant Dan calmly turned to Forrest and said, "I never thanked you for saving my life."

"He never actually said so," said Forrest, who was narrating his life story, "but I think he made his peace with God."[5] Lieutenant Dan's life changed the day he was willing to wrestle with the power of God and the life he never wanted.

If God is powerful, that means He is in your circumstances. That does not mean God ordains evil, but He does allow human freedom. And human freedom permits human sin that creates human suffering.

Acknowledging God's power means admitting that someone is actually in control, and that truth may enable you to acknowledge your anger and confusion—at people, at circumstances, and ultimately at God. And honesty is truly the only way to healing and peace. Every issue you have in this season is ultimately a question of theology—what you believe about God. And what you believe about Him is everything. If you are in pain and believe that God is powerful, you will have issues with Him. But if you don't believe that God is able to re-create and redeem, if you don't believe His hand is at work even in the rain clouds and nuclear warheads, then all hope is truly lost.

Then there is the belief that God is good, which brings us to the thorniest obstacle of all: thinking that goes like this . . .

If God is good, He must not be powerful because if He was, He wouldn't allow this to happen.

If God is powerful, He must not be good—or He wouldn't allow this to happen.

Knowing God: The Tension of Opposing Forces

God's very nature includes His complete power and complete love. God's power—His moral perfection—without love would lead to shame, distance, condemnation. Love without power would lead to a weak, sentimental experience. But our minds have a very hard time holding these two qualities together as completely true when they often feel in opposition to one another.

In situations that exceed our mental abilities, we tend to lean into simplistic answers: "Just have faith." "Make peace." "God is enough." And while we do need faith and peace and the belief that God is enough, we do not have to check our brains at the door in order to trust.

At first glance, God's power and God's love may seem like a paradox. A paradox is a statement that seems to be contradictory but leads to a deeper underlying meaning: "This is the beginning of the end," or "If I know one thing, it's that I know nothing." Paradox uses language to bring fresh perspective and to provoke deeper thought. The apostle Paul loved a good paradox. "For when I am weak, then I am strong" and "sorrowful, yet always rejoicing"[6] are both great examples.

But when it comes to the quest to understand God's power and love, we are not talking about two words that seem in opposition to one another—they are two realities that seem in opposition to each other. That is not a paradox; it's an antinomy. Now hang with me as we get a bit nerdy together, because this has immediate and direct ramifications for the wrestling you must face as you enter your unexpected season. As opposed to a paradox, an *antinomy* is defined as:

a. a contradiction between two apparently equally valid principles

b. a fundamental and apparently unresolvable conflict or contradiction[7]

In *Evangelism and the Sovereignty of God*, J. I. Packer also uses the word *apparent* to illustrate how it works in our experience of God: "It is an apparent incompatibility between two apparent truths. An antinomy exists when a pair of principles stand side by side, seemingly irreconcilable, yet both undeniable."[8] Why does this matter? Because unexpected seasons of loss, suffering, or change force these questions:

"If God is so good, why did He allow this to happen?"
"If God is good, then am I being punished for messing up in some way?"
"If God is in control, why does what I do even matter?"
"If God is powerful, why would He allow _____ to happen to me/my loved one?"

To call these situations paradoxes is to cheapen the lived experience of being caught between two truths that don't line up, as if it's just a clever turn of phrase designed to get our attention. But all the attention in the world won't resolve this tension, particularly when we're encouraged to ease it by leaning one way or the other: either overemphasizing God's sovereignty—"God is in control so He must have willed this for you"—or overemphasizing human responsibility—"You really messed that up; you'd better try harder next time." We may find ourselves so tangled in this tension that we resolve it by walking away, leaving the faith altogether.

Applying a big word like *antinomy* to the dilemma actually brings comfort. It means that others before us have acknowledged, studied, and put words to our lived experience. There is even comfort in saying "God's power and God's love sometimes seem to directly contradict one another," or "God's sovereignty and human responsibility seem to directly contradict each other."

As Packer aptly states, "An antinomy is neither dispensable nor comprehensible. It is not a figure of speech, but an observed relation between two statements of fact. . . . We may be sure that they all find their reconciliation in the mind and counsel of God."[9] To put it plainly, the only way to find resolution in this life is to acknowledge that the finitude of our minds will keep us from finding resolution. So that very clichéd suggestion to "just have faith" gets at exactly what we need, but finding our faith in the midst of contradictions isn't something that happens overnight. It's a journey, a fight, a surrender, an acceptance. It's the very best thing that can happen in our unexpected seasons, but it's also the very hardest thing. One of my readers shared this:

> I am still learning much more deeply what it means to trust in God. For a long time I was functioning under the mentality that things were hard because I wasn't trusting God enough, and if I could just say the right thing, or make the right choice at the right moment, that my problems would resolve and dissipate. I was treating my faith like an escape room puzzle to be solved.

If a God who is both all-powerful and all-loving doesn't seem to match your experience in this hard season, may I gently ask you to consider whether it is possible that somewhere toward eternity these two qualities do intersect? Could it simply be they coexist in a way you cannot fully grasp in the here and now?

Here's one piece of evidence for this argument: Whenever a person creates anything, pieces of that person will be in whatever they create. As I wrote this book, I included my own experiences in it—parts of me are here. If you paint a picture, part of you—your brushstroke, the way you interpret a scene—will always be in the picture. So if we see what appears to us as contradictions in our

Creator, is it possible that He left us clues in His creation that two apparent contradictions can both be true? Packer points out that He did—in the form of light.[10] Here's the thing about light: It baffles even the smartest among us. Physicists argue whether, on the subatomic level, light is a particle or a wave. Well, as it turns out, it's both. But particles and waves are completely different from one another. A particle is distinct; a wave is diffuse. A particle bounces off another particle; a wave can join or change directions or integrate with another wave. Particles of sand never function like waves of water.

And yet.

Light is both particles and waves. Sometimes it behaves like a particle; sometimes it acts like a wave. We have no choice but to be reconciled to the fact that we don't actually fully understand how it works—we just have evidence that it does. That is an antinomy that you encounter every time you flip on the light switch, whether you know it or not. So is it possible that the nature of God, Creator of light, Creator of you, whose ways are actually higher than your ways, can coexist in *seeming* opposites too?

What relevance does this have for you in this season that you never signed up for? It means that you may have questions that can't be answered within the limits of your understanding. It means you'll have to accept holding together God's love and God's power, God's sovereignty and our human responsibility, without fully reconciling them through your intelligence alone. You'll have to be okay when people around you, including and especially pastors, try to make God about one or the other in a way that you know doesn't get to the heart of the issue.

Our unexpected seasons always invite us to go deeper than black and white, cause and effect, heroes and villains. Unexpected seasons invite us into the mystery, into places where peace comes only from full surrender to what we can't understand, with full comfort in what God has clearly given us. Wrestling, lamenting, and even shaking your fist at God can bring you to a place of peace and purpose like you've never known before. This is something we can only *know*—a place where truth and experience meet. When your weakness, doubt, and hurt are fully exposed, you recognize that God stays with you even there. You discover that what He wanted all along was you. At your worst and weakest, He is there with His love.

One of the great comforts in my unexpected season was the number of people—some longtime friends, some whom I barely knew—who told me of their own unexpected seasons. They were able to be guiding lights along the way, beckoning and even pushing me forward when I felt like there was no place to go. Not one of them could explain why God had done what He'd done in their lives. But they could testify to His love and His presence. In their eyes and in their stories, I saw a shimmer of something beautiful and eternal. I think that shimmer is what a deep inner trust looks like from the outside.

This acceptance of the mystery can make the higher ways of God comforting, not conflicting. Maybe you will come to share the sentiment of the famous nineteenth-century preacher C. H. Spurgeon, who was asked if he could reconcile the opposing truths of divine sovereignty and human responsibility to each other: "'I wouldn't try,' he replied; 'I never reconcile friends.'"[11]

So what can we know? We know what God has given us to know:

Do not be afraid.
God is here.
God has plans to accomplish good for you and through you.

A PRAYER FOR TAKING IT ONE DAY AT A TIME

God of light and Father of mine,

Remind me of the truth today
as I am having a hard time believing but
*   need to hear:*

I am resilient.
I am armed with hope.
I am coping.
I am putting one foot in front of the other.

You are with me.
Your strength is enough.
Your comfort is abundant.
You walk with me every step of the way.

May every light I see today remind me
that I can trust
even when I don't understand.

Amen.

Potiphar put him in charge of his household, and he entrusted to his care everything he owned. . . .

The warden put Joseph in charge of all those held in the prison, and he was made responsible for all that was done there. . . .

Pharaoh said to Joseph, "I hereby put you in charge of the whole land of Egypt."

GENESIS 39:4, 22; 41:41

CHAPTER 7

TRUST THE OPPORTUNITY

*Do not forget to show hospitality to strangers, for by so doing some
people have shown hospitality to angels without knowing it.*

HEBREWS 13:2

Drowning.

That's the metaphor that best describes how I felt in the weeks
and months after I'd left my work and the community that had
loved me, shaped me, and defined me to a fault for over twenty
years. I chose to leave, knowing it was the right thing to do and
that God had most certainly and definitely called me out.

I had spent months receiving counsel before making the
change; I pleaded with God and so deeply desired a different way.
As I contemplated this move, one of my wise counselors told me
repeatedly, "You'll know when you know. And if you don't know,
it's not time." I heeded that advice until it became clear that this
wasn't a change I was really *choosing*—it was a necessary next step.
In his book *The Making of a Leader*, Robert Clinton calls this season *negative preparation*, a time when God might use painful experiences to free a person to enter the next season.[1] It was painful,

all right. And it didn't feel freeing. It felt like fleeing. It felt like escaping through a dark underwater tunnel with no knowledge of where that tunnel would lead.

Even though I could return to the story and find the marked places of obedience within it, this did not change the experience of waking up each morning like I was coming up for air, still trying to swim out of that dark tunnel. I doubted everything I believed by 10 a.m. My mind was constantly trying to resolve the loop of contradictions between the choice I'd made and what it cost, and I was exhausted and depressed by the effort.

How could God will something that felt so bad? How could everything going wrong be considered right by God? I wanted to hibernate. Maybe I could pull the covers over my head and pass this winter in my soul by sleeping through it. Looking back, I see the graciousness of God in preventing me from doing that. I still had kids who wanted breakfast, there were car pools to drive and work assignments with due dates. Though I couldn't shake the feeling that I was drowning, I couldn't give myself over to it either.

I remember one particular conversation I had with my spiritual director while I was lying in bed (thank you, video counseling). She invited me to consider some self-care practices that kept my head just above water while the waves receded. She forced me to action when I wanted to stay paralyzed. She held out a light, and that light came in the form of journaling my honest prayers, forcing myself to list out what I was grateful for, giving myself permission to be angry and sad without rushing through it. It looked like weighted blankets and naps and cooking meals for my family. It looked like just saying yes to the next thing, which resulted in my taking on many unusual and odd jobs (more on that later). Sometimes even when our heart isn't in it, our feet can help us find the way forward.

Getting stuck is a natural response in our unexpected seasons. We want to fight the world, to hold on to the hurt and grief and to force time to stop until everything is made right again—or we long to pull the covers over our heads as a way to tune out what feels unmanageable. But neither response will actually give us what we need in this season: the ability to stay present and engaged exactly where we are. We have to simply claim that even today is "the day that the LORD has made," and it's possible that we can "rejoice and be glad in it" (Psalm 118:24, ESV). Since God made the day, He will also make rejoicing in Him possible. "I will see the goodness of the LORD in the land of the living" (Psalm 27:13).

What we need in our unexpected seasons is the ability to stay present and engaged exactly where we are.

When I look back on the sharpest points of grief, I discover that God was running ahead of me all the while. In those first few months, I preached at churches, I officiated a wedding, I went to the hospital when babies were born, and I rushed to the ER when other babies were sick. I just kept being a minister even without a ministry home. I hardly even remember that season; it was such a blur of grief. But looking back, I can see that God was still opening doors, still shining a little light down into that deep underwater tunnel. I can see His intent—giving me just enough light to keep stepping forward but not so much that I could sidestep the pain.

Only a month after leaving my role, a church called me out of the blue, inviting me to be an interim pastor of sorts while they were in their senior pastor search. Saratoga Federated is located in a little enclave in the Bay Area of California, at the foot of the Santa Cruz Mountains. For the first season after leaving my church, I found myself plucked out and away from my familiar Sunday routine, a full three thousand miles from the place our family had worshiped for over twenty years. Sunday after Sunday, I just happened to be somewhere else—and only God would know how healing, how restoring, how deeply right it was for me to fly for hours to spend solitude in the redwoods on Saturday and then preach the Word to the most receptive, warm, appreciative little community of believers on Sunday. Little lights in a dark tunnel.

What I've come to understand through all of this pain is that God's goodness is not for tomorrow, it's not for next year, and it's certainly not reserved only for heaven. It's for today. Today is the day that you can rejoice in God. It's possible no matter the circumstance, and it's the unique opportunity we are given in this season. It's one thing to know the goodness of God when everything already feels pretty good. It's an entirely different experience to know and experience the goodness of God in a season you would never sign up for. God's goodness when you are at your worst is one of the ways you begin to trust Him more deeply even when you return to your best. Trusting the opportunities today is the invitation. Believing in the goodness of God is the quest. In the midst of all that occupies your mind and emotions in this season, God still calls you to action. And action will buoy you up. You are never done being useful in God's hands.

Joseph's persistent belief that God was always working through him would eventually lead him to his next chapter: Pharaoh's court. But I want to slow down and stay where we've been—in the interlude between the day Joseph rightly interpreted the cupbearer's dream and the two years after that when the cupbearer forgot all about him. Let's picture Joseph finally lying down to rest in his prison cell, 730 days after his last interaction with the cupbearer, and more days than he could count since his last time with his father. And as we imagine that moment, let's consider what it looked like to trust the opportunities God gave. For unbeknownst to Joseph, Pharaoh was also lying in his bed, where he was troubled by weird and detailed dreams.

Joseph had now been gone from his family for at least eleven years. He'd moved through his late teen years and into adulthood. He'd experienced his twenties as a slave, a house steward, and a prisoner. Yet one theme remained through it all: God was with him. God showed him favor. And that's not all—Joseph kept showing up. In every setting, Joseph showed up with humility, with presence, and with skill. He showed up believing that his life mattered and that the way he lived each day was important. He bore the test of loss, holding on to his stories and his dream. He showed up for the test of integrity with Potiphar's wife by rebuffing her advances. He showed up for the test of humility in the way he conducted himself in the prison, serving the warden and caring for the king's prisoners while also giving glory to God for everything he had.

Joseph cooperated with God's favor. He didn't hold it in contempt by ignoring or denying that his life was important. Even when in prison, he still showed up like his life counted, like he could be used by God no matter what.

I wonder what it would be like today, in whatever prison you feel you are in, if you showed up believing that this day is not just another day of languishing in a spiritual waiting room. That this day is about to bloom with opportunity. That even though your opportunities look incredibly different from what you expected, even though they're not what you would choose or even wish on your enemy, the favor of God is still with you, and this day matters. *Let us rejoice and be glad in it.*

No Time like the Present

Because Joseph was present to God and what He was doing around him, he knew the Lord could use him anytime and anywhere. This gave him a particular perspective that went beyond seconds, minutes, hours, and days. Time is a weird construct, one that we often limit to what we see on the clock. Think of all of the ways we engage—and are in conflict—with it. We are constantly trying to "save time" (impossible), or we fret because we are "behind the times" (also impossible). We are looking for "spare time"; we don't want to "waste time"; or we have to "kill time" to get to the next thing. We are in a wrestling match with time—on the one hand, it seems to limit us, while on the other, we are obsessed with trying to use it to get what we want, when we want it.

In the Bible, though, *time* has more than one meaning. There are two distinct Greek words that appear in the Bible to refer to time. The first, *chronos*, is where we get the word *chronology*—meaning a timeline. *Chronos* time is typically what we measure in minutes and hours. It's the linear expression we've placed on our earthly experience. *Chronos* time is how we know that Joseph was seventeen when he was sold into slavery, thirty when he was elevated to lead Egypt, and forty before he saw his brothers again. At some point, *chronos* time will also be how you describe your unexpected season: It took three years to move on. . . . seven years to forgive . . . fourteen years of trying . . . twenty-two years until the dream was realized.

The other Greek word the Bible uses for time is *kairos*. This word for time is generally about moments of opportunity, those snapshots in our lives that capture a critical juncture that will impact the future. However, *kairos* moments are often only fully realized in retrospect. It is only later in our stories that we are able to look back and say *Ah!—that was the moment.* It's that first conversation, that happenstance meeting, that day you took a different route to work and what happened because of it. *Kairos* moments help define our destiny, and they are critical intersections as we live out our calling to bear witness to the grace of Jesus, to carry the kingdom of God with us, to allow blessing to flow through us in whatever plot twist God has next. Perhaps even now you can think back to one or two of these moments in your own story.

Maybe one of those *kairos* moments has led you to the season you are in now. If it's not what you expected, you may have begun to doubt that you heard God right. After all, why in the world would He have brought you this far to dump you in the garbage heap that is now your life? Yet if we had encountered twenty-nine-year-old Joseph, unshaven, dirty, and forgotten, sleeping on a pallet in the corner of a cell in a dark dungeon, we would assume he hadn't experienced any *kairos* moments lately. But we have the benefit of knowing the rest of the story. We know that in this moment, Pharaoh was having a dream. We know that tomorrow, Joseph would be remembered and needed. Tomorrow, every single moment leading to this point would matter:

- the moment the Midianites encountered Joseph's brothers and bought Joseph from them,
- which led him to a slave's position in Potiphar's household, where he gained Potiphar's favor and trust,
- which left Joseph to attend to his master's affairs alone in the house where Potiphar's wife framed him after he rebuffed her advances, unjustly sending him to prison,
- which is where he was when the cupbearer needed his dream interpreted,
- which meant that two years after the cupbearer forgot all about Joseph, he knew exactly where to find him the morning Pharaoh woke up in desperate need of someone to interpret his dreams.

Taken individually and in *chronos* time, these moments don't seem like *kairos* opportunities. Other than the one time in eleven years that Joseph had a moment of hope after the cupbearer's release from prison (which immediately faded), every other moment listed was a moment of loss or suffering. Imagine how these moments must have seared into Joseph's heart, seeming to take him so far from his experience as a favored son with big dreams! And yet. Every one of these moments mattered and led to the next. It's often only in hindsight that *kairos* moments become evident. Maybe that's why *kairos* moments are always about what's good today, what matters today, what you can do today—trusting that what happens today has eternal significance for tomorrow.

This kind of expectancy carries an urgent hope:

As God's co-workers we urge you not to receive God's grace in vain. For he says,

*"In the time [kairos] of my favor I heard you,
and in the day of salvation I helped you."*

*I tell you, now is the time [kairos] of God's favor, now is the
day of salvation.*

2 CORINTHIANS 6:1-2

In the ultimate of breakthrough moments, Jesus entered into our reality. He entered into life just like we do—with all of the joy and wonder and love, and all the sadness, discouragement, and pain. He took on all of it so that the power of darkness could be broken for us. He broke His body for us so that all that is broken is not lost and useless. Jesus came, fully God and fully man, to do what we could never do for ourselves. He took it all upon Himself, took it to the grave, and then rose up victorious in the ultimate act of redemption. We get to experience the *now* of salvation. If God can redeem our souls, He can certainly redeem our days, no matter how hard those days might feel right now.

Oh, my friend, how I long to be with you right now, to trace the story of your hardship and listen as you discover the *kairos* moments embedded within your own chapters![2] How I want you not to give up hope even though you are desperate for this season to pass! How Joseph must have struggled and suffered during those many years, yet he kept showing up for the opportunities in front of him. Even though most did not lead him where he expected—and in fact, there were many times when, looking in from the outside, people would have concluded, "Certainly he's being punished!"—he kept showing up.

Now was the time of the Lord's favor in Joseph's life, even when that favor looked like a dark prison cell and more years of waiting than any of us could imagine dealing with! And yet—God was present. What a reminder to all of us not to judge so quickly about what God is up to in our lives or the lives of others. God is always at work and *now* is the time of His favor.

On the night before Joseph was called into Pharaoh's court, he didn't yet know he would never return to his cell. Joseph was about to be given the assignment of a lifetime. The weight of responsibility for an entire nation would soon rest upon his shoulders. We understand that this next step in Joseph's life *still* wouldn't be the full realization of his dream and that there was more to come. But on this night, in this dungeon, Joseph believed only that every day was another opportunity and that how he showed up mattered. And because of his faithfulness over the years, tomorrow would be the day when all of his experiences from all the places he never wanted to be would matter more than he could have ever dreamed.

Nowhere by Accident

Pete, one of my great friends and mentors, loves to give this benediction: "You go nowhere by accident. Wherever you go, God is sending you." This prayer was first delivered by Richard Halverson, former chaplain of the US Senate, and it is a fitting summary of Joseph's life. Trusting the opportunity means to believe that, whether you are in a prison or a palace, you are not there by accident, or even worse, as punishment. In fact, your presence is not even neutral—you've been placed there intentionally, for a purpose. God has intentions for your life even in this season, even now.

If you learn nothing else from the story of Joseph, don't forget that every chapter in his story mattered for the chapter that followed. His redemption didn't happen quickly, it didn't happen easily, but it happened.

It was not an accident that the cupbearer forgot all about Joseph. It was not an accident that Joseph's unexpected season was prolonged by two years. And in the ongoing antinomy between God's sovereignty and human responsibility, we see how intentional God is and yet how much it matters that we respond to opportunities before us.

God's covenant blessing carried Abraham, Isaac, and Jacob through their failings. His blessings continued despite their mistakes. But with Joseph, we see God's covenant blessings moving forward because of Joseph's faithfulness and obedience. He displayed moral courage in ways his fathers before him did not. Both Abraham and Isaac would not stand up to powerful kings who pursued their wives. But Joseph stood up to a powerful wife who pursued him. Commentators call this part of Genesis a "great reversal"—the breaking of generational patterns of infidelity and family animosity that characterized the generations before Joseph.[3] (More on that as the story continues.) But the reversal started while Joseph was still enslaved, while he was still waiting. That reversal began one opportunity at a time.

This is the point in the story where I wish we could ask Joseph what we all want to know: What sustained him? How did he keep showing up with peace and purpose? How I wish we could have Joseph color in the missing days and weeks with details from his side of the story! But instead, we'll have to pay attention to every detail in the narrative, knowing that each one is important, and use them as a set of clues to help us understand how to do more than barely survive our season but rejoice in the day the Lord has made. We can learn how to respond faithfully and purposefully to the *kairos* moments in our lives.

In Joseph's season and our own, trusting the opportunity actually flows in three directions:

Upward: the opportunity to engage God
Inward: the opportunity to engage our inner world
Outward: the opportunity to engage the world around us

Let's examine what each looked like for Joseph and what each can look like for us.

Upward: engaging God

God is a quiet figure in Joseph's story. God didn't appear as a smoking firepot, as He did to Abraham (Genesis 15:17). He didn't speak audibly, as He did with Isaac (Genesis 26). He didn't appear as a mysterious figure, wrestling with Jacob (Genesis 32:22-32). These men encountered God's visible presence. With Joseph, God was the unseen hand advancing the clock in Joseph's life. He was the silent influence as Joseph moved through palace and prison.

The Lord appears in Joseph's story only when Joseph mentioned Him and when others noticed God's presence in Joseph's life. For instance, when the king's servants told him their dreams, Joseph used the opportunity to engage upward: "Do not interpretations belong to God?" before engaging outward: "Tell me your dreams" (Genesis 40:8).

Such an upward orientation feels counterintuitive when our lives are full of difficulties. We normally assume we need to focus on the problems in order to relieve our pain. All throughout Scripture, however, we are told that when we worship God, our perspective on pain will change.[4] As one of you told me with a shrug when reflecting on your stance toward God during your own unexpected season: "Well, I just praised Him anyway."

Praise Him anyway.

I often find that in my deepest times of despair, I need the words of others to realign my heart upward. The Psalms are the place where lament and worship freely coexist; where I can acknowledge the trouble and darkness that so often surround me while also embracing the light and goodness of God's peace, mercy, and love.

I have a simple upward practice: I read the Psalms until a verse or phrase stands out on the page. Sometimes it's the first line; sometimes it's a few chapters in. Then I write that one verse or phrase into my journal. The physical act of copying the verse in my own hand is a way to claim the truth, promise, or encouragement. I then write a short prayer underneath that, asking God for whatever comes to mind from that verse. Rather than allowing my flip-flopping heart or fickle emotions to lead my time with God, I start from His Word so that I can posture my soul upward, and then work inward from there. This exercise is not flashy, time-consuming, or particularly creative. But it's consistent, a habit built over time that aligns me with the presence and peace of God.

Inward: engaging the soul

One reason our inner world matters is because we are often unaware of how easily we can dwell on the past or be anxious about the future, completely checked out from where we actually are. There is only one way to fully engage with our current opportunity: We have to be present today. As my friend Jeanne Stevens said so beautifully on my podcast when I interviewed her about her book *What's Here Now?*, "If we are rehashing the past or rehearsing the future, we can't receive the present."[5] Only people who live in the present can serve well, notice well, and engage with what God is doing in the *kairos* moments all around them. And to be present is to be at peace in the moment—whether happy or hard. Engaging inward is a simple practice of checking in on yourself and adjusting your perspective to stay in the present.

One of my favorite things to do when I'm working with leadership teams is to help them connect inward. As a practice, I teach them a posture—putting their hands together in a prayer position, thumbs touching the center of their chests. This is a heart posture, where we are physically connecting our hands and hearts, reminding our bodies that we are not just mechanically surviving this life but that our souls can dwell with us in the present moment. In this position, we can acknowledge our needs and ask God to meet them in a way that allows us to be an instrument for His plans and purposes. Only when we are focused upward and then inward are we properly aligned to engage outwardly with the opportunities in front of us.

Though the Joseph narrative doesn't directly tell us about his inner world, his humility and dependence on God suggest that Joseph desired to walk closely with Him. Psalm 105 gives us a window into how this time of waiting shaped Joseph's inner life: "Until the time came to fulfill his dreams, the LORD tested Joseph's character" (Psalm 105:19, NLT).

Outward: engaging the world

Recently I had coffee with a friend who is living in a long, unexpected season of singleness—framing and reframing her life around a dream that has not happened in her timing and may not happen at all. "I've been living for a while now like I'm only going to be happy with big changes," she told me. "But changes aren't coming. So instead of being so worried about what I need to change, I decided I need to fully engage with exactly what I have right now." She went on to share what a difference that's made in the joy she experiences every day. Turns out, she discovered that her circumstances aren't nearly as painful since she decided to fully live into them, without ruminating on the things she can't control or change.

When Joseph spoke with the cupbearer and the baker, he was not wrapped up in his own pain. Because he trusted God, he had humility, and that humility allowed him to be present. And the present is where we notice things. One morning, he asked his two fellow prisoners, "Why are your faces so sad today?" (Genesis 40:7, NASB). Notice this small but important detail: Only people fully engaged in the present and confident that their presence matters will notice something as small as a facial expression and then try to do something to help.

What does it look like to be present wherever you are? I'm

reminded of a temporary exhibit that once stopped at the science museum near our house. It focused on the marvel of the human body and included many interactive displays designed to measure all kinds of human performance. My highly competitive children acted like bulls at a rodeo, galloping and bucking from one exhibit to the other, testing vertical leaps and balance and vocal pitch and grip strength. But one exhibit—a reaction timer—was particularly fascinating. One by one they stood in front of a massive panel of lights, and the machine recorded the time it took them to touch the panel after it lit up. The display was so large that my kids couldn't fully focus on any one area, so they had to diffuse their focus across all the panels and trust their peripheral vision to alert them when a light flashed. I was transfixed as my kids stood in front of those panels. It was like watching puppies focused on a treat: their eyes wide, arms open, their whole selves expectant. They were completely engaged—in their bodies, focused not on yesterday or tomorrow—simply attentive in the moment. This is what being present looks like.

Kairos Living

In your current season, what would it be like to watch God with that same focus: upward in worship; inward in reflection, confession, and supplication; and then outward to the world, eyes wide, arms open, your whole self expectant for the *kairos* moments around you? What if you saw your unexpected season not as a trial to get through without drowning, but as an opportunity to keep your eyes on Jesus so you could learn to walk on water?

> What if you saw your unexpected season not as a trial to get through without drowning, but as an opportunity to keep your eyes on Jesus so you could learn to walk on water?

What does trusting the opportunities in this way look like? Here are insights some of you have shared with me:

This season has been so lonely, but I think it's because the only way I could actually get to the deep stuff that needed to be dealt with was by God removing some of those relationships.

This was an opportunity for God to shift my focus entirely to Him in a way I never had before. This was Him inviting me into a relationship I wasn't aware I didn't have before. I learned what peace that passes all understanding actually looks and feels like. I learned to walk in joy. I've always known that nothing is more important than the purpose God gave me, but I learned that that purpose is more important than the job in which I perform it. For me, there is no such thing as a permanent job anymore. There is only what God has for me to do whether I am in a place a long while or a short while.

When I had my miscarriage, every day was hard for the first month. I talked it over with my husband, and that processing helped a lot. We found ourselves growing closer in a way that I don't think would have happened otherwise. I trusted him more, and we made more time for connecting.

These are our *kairos* moments. Even though we may feel as if we are only crawling along in faith, God is creating moments of opportunity, drawing us upward and inward, and then releasing us outward so that we might be a blessing to others even in our darkest times.

When the cupbearer finally remembered the fellow prisoner who'd interpreted his dream, when Joseph was summoned up from the dungeon to stand in front of Pharaoh, Joseph didn't do anything new. He did exactly what he'd been doing since he'd been ripped from his family many years before: He gave glory to God. When asked if he could interpret Pharaoh's dreams, he replied, "It has nothing to do with me; God will give Pharaoh an answer for his own good" (Genesis 41:16, NASB). He focused everyone's attention upward. Although we don't know the details, we can be sure Joseph managed his own inward condition in a way that allowed him to be present outwardly, and then he trusted the opportunities God gave him.

And once again, he interpreted the dream rightly.

The eleven years of experience he gained in a season he'd never wanted was about to become vitally important. For what Joseph couldn't have known as a teenager with a dream was that God had begun preparing him for his greatest assignment yet. As a young man he managed Potiphar's household and, later, Pharaoh's prison. He spent years honing his skills in managing tasks and people and building strategy, impressing both Potiphar and the prison warden. And now, while standing before Pharaoh after interpreting his dreams, Joseph was able to offer a sound business strategy:

Famine is coming.
It's a moment of opportunity.
Lead wisely for the next seven years, and you'll be powerful,
  secure, prosperous.
Lead poorly, and you'll doom your country to starvation.
Choose someone capable to lead.

Hours earlier, when Joseph woke up in the corner of a dungeon, in dirty clothes and with an unshaven face, it likely seemed to him like the start of just one more monotonous day. For him it was another occasion to simply trust the opportunities in front of him. Yet on that very same day, his fortunes reversed. For it was Joseph's very orientation toward God that qualified him in Pharaoh's eyes: "This proposal pleased Pharaoh and all his servants. And Pharaoh said to his servants, 'Can we find a man like this, *in whom is the Spirit of God?'* Then Pharaoh said to Joseph, 'Since God has shown you all this, there is none so discerning and wise as you are'" (Genesis 41:37-39, esv, emphasis added).

The cast-off kid, the teenage slave, the wrongly accused steward, the humble jail servant—he was now in charge of Egypt!

A PRAYER FOR WHEN YOU ARE WAITING

God of time,

I confess that it often feels like You are late,
or I am early,
or we are out of step.
I wonder how much longer I can stay here,
for my hope is failing,
and my strength is fading,
and my steps are heavy with the burden of my
*   own doubt.*
Would You give me a vision for today that matches
*   Your desires:*
eyes to see opportunities;
hands willing to pray, serve, embrace, hold;
and a heart that trusts
right here in this today with You.

Amen.

Before the years of famine came, two sons were born to Joseph by Asenath daughter of Potiphera, priest of On. Joseph named his firstborn Manasseh and said, "It is because God has made me forget all my trouble and all my father's household." The second son he named Ephraim and said, "It is because God has made me fruitful in the land of my suffering."

GENESIS 41:50-52

CHAPTER 8

TRUST THE TEARS

There is a sacredness in tears. They are not the mark of
weakness, but of power. They speak more eloquently than ten
thousand tongues. They are the messengers of overwhelming
grief, of deep contrition, and of unspeakable love.

ATTRIBUTED TO WASHINGTON IRVING

Sometimes after I give a message at a worship service or retreat, someone will approach me and begin crying. Without fail, they look embarrassed and surprised. "I don't know why I'm crying . . . ," they all say. But I like the tears because tears mean truth. Tears mean that the person is facing reality, even when that reality is difficult. Starting my vocational ministry career as a therapist certainly helped me get well-acquainted with other people's tears, to appreciate them so deeply for what they represent. But strangely, that's never made it any easier when I'm the one who begins to weep. There's something so vulnerable, so out of control, so uncomfortably real about tears. There's something about being overcome with so much emotion. Maybe it frightens us to know that we feel so deeply. Maybe it scares us to discover just how much we care. Maybe we are worried that once we open ourselves up to whatever grief or pain or even love that's behind those tears, we will never be the same.

And maybe that's exactly why tears are so important.

By this time, we all know how Joseph's story turns out. But because of that, we can miss the full experience, the depths of what God is teaching us as we immerse ourselves in the very real twists and turns of this story. I think that's why noticing the grief that fills Joseph's life is so helpful when it comes to fully embracing our own unexpected seasons. When we look closely, we see that his story is marked by all kinds of tears from beginning to end: tears of mourning, tears of desperation, tears of loss, tears of joy. The first tears we see, however, are at the beginning of our Joseph story and belong to Jacob. After the other brothers presented Jacob with Joseph's beautiful, bloodstained robe, leading their father to believe Joseph had been killed by a wild animal, Jacob cried, "I will continue to mourn until I join my son in the grave" (Genesis 37:35). Apparently, Joseph came by his big emotions naturally.

The Bible is relatively quiet about Joseph's emotional experience during the first thirteen years of his captivity, but that doesn't mean we have no clues about how he felt and how he handled his loss. After being released from prison to rule at Pharaoh's right hand, we see clues in Scripture that illuminate the way Joseph experienced the narrative of his life. In ancient times, even more than now, the names parents gave to their children had great significance. Joseph's father, Jacob, had his name changed by God to Israel, which meant "you struggled with God and with men and won" (Genesis 32:28, CEB). When Rachel, the true love of Jacob's life, finally became pregnant after years of infertility and strife between her and Jacob's other wives and mistresses, she named her firstborn son Joseph, which means "increase." Before she could celebrate what God had done for her, she was already impatient in her desire for another son.[1]

Names were considered prophetic, harbingers of what was to come. But when Joseph began his life as a husband and father, he did something different. He named his sons through his pain and as a memorial to the past.

The greatest good he could put on these years of pain was expressed in the name he gave his first son, Manasseh: "God has made me forget." He named his second son Ephraim: "God has made me fruitful in the land of my suffering." (Genesis 41:51-52). Joseph was not celebrating his rise to the top. He was not looking back and making it all okay. He was not pretending that success in Egypt was the blessing he had always wanted. He wasn't settling on aspirational names for his sons, like some famous athletes have today: Yourhighness Morgan, Wonderful Terrific Monds Jr., Commander King. Joseph marked his journey by naming his sons "Forget" and "Fruitful Suffering."

As we continue the journey through Joseph's story, the Scriptures give us *seven* separate accounts of Joseph weeping *after* his reversal of fortune. Joseph is a man who knows how to lament, how to grieve, and how to connect his heart to his story even (and especially) in the painful places of loss.

As much as we desire to live into peace, love, and happiness, loss is inevitable and as much a part of our stories as any triumphs God has prepared for us. To follow Christ is to experience joy, yes, but also suffering. The task before us is to become men and women of faith who embrace the mystery of hearts that are big enough to hold both joy and sorrow, hearts that allow themselves to be broken and put back together again, over and over.

So far, we've hung on to the hope of the promises of God's great blessing upon us:

Do not be afraid.
God is here.
God has plans to accomplish good for you and through you.

And from that place of assurance, we walk bravely forward into the darkness of our loss.

I recently visited the 9/11 Memorial in New York City. The memorial features two massive reflecting pools, each with a square-shaped hole in the center. Black granite fills the space where the Twin Towers used to stand, with an endless fountain spilling into the center cavities. The names of those killed that day are etched around the walls of the pools, a constant and ongoing reminder of the darkness and loss felt by those who loved them. It seems we all have similar holes somewhere in our own stories. Your grief may be deep and recognizable to those around you, or it might be private and invisible. Being a human is hard. We go through trials, betrayals, and troubles of all kinds. Grief is inevitable—even Jesus experienced it. Yet this is the unique and comforting and powerful truth of Christianity: Although we grieve, we do not have to grieve like those without hope (1 Thessalonians 4:13).

As we spend time together in this book, you may be realizing how deep your grief truly is and how little you have worked through it. If so, these pages may seem to give you more pain than hope, especially if you have unprocessed memories and emotions that rush forward when you open the door of your soul just a tiny crack. If that is the case, I want you to take heart and know that it is possible to step into the darkness and emerge on the other side. If loss is your primary experience in this season, I recommend to you the beautiful book *A Grace Disguised.* Author and professor Jerry Sittser wrote the book after his wife, mother, and four-year-old daughter died when their car was struck by a drunk driver who had crossed into their lane. In an instant, he became a single father to three surviving young children. He wrote the book to help others see what it means to absorb and then grow through grief, even the most unimaginable losses. Your story might be dramatic and tragic, like Jerry's. Or it might be made up of accumulated losses over time. Either way, as Sittser says, "All losses are bad, only bad in different ways."[2]

A while back I posted a picture of the books I'd been reading about grief, loss, and the importance of our tears, asking about your practices during seasons of sorrow. (I'll share those in the "Practices of Lament" section at the end of this chapter.) What struck me was how many of you simply responded, "I'm looking for help with this." So let's consider how God meets us in times of grief and how we can move through our loss—no matter the source—with grace and courage.

Defining Grief

Embracing and honoring your grief is the final stage in learning to trust God in your painful, unexpected season, and it's the longest part of the journey. As you mourn, it's critical to engage with God about what you've lost, what you miss, and what you grieve. Even if the loss is something you chose or something that's ultimately good (like your children growing up), and even if what you've left behind comes with many new and good things, it's still loss. It's still the end of a season, the death of a dream, the loss of a relationship.

Grief comes to all of us in different forms in our "not what we signed up for" seasons. We often think grief follows only the experience of losing someone in the definitive, destructive pattern of death. Whether it be our parent, a friend—even a pet—the gap they leave behind is a permanent hole that can never be filled. But grief is reserved not just for death but for losses of all kinds. Grief is never simple—it's often a mix of conflicting emotions. Perhaps that's why tears, too, are never simple. Tears are an outward expression of our strong emotions—something beyond our ability to internalize. Researchers theorize that tears are made to signal to others our need for connection. Perhaps that's why weeping is so vulnerable—it's a universal human signal indicating our need for help.[3]

Consider Joseph's episodes of weeping to think about what our tears can represent:

- After many years in Egypt, Joseph met his brothers again, but they did not recognize him. Joseph wept when he understood what they said to one another in Hebrew—and knew they had not forgotten about him but in fact felt guilty about what they had done (Genesis 42:24).

- Joseph wept when he met his younger brother, Benjamin, perhaps overcome by both the joy of knowing he was alive and the sorrow of having lost so many years with him (Genesis 43:30).

- Joseph broke down when he revealed himself to his brothers. "He wept so loudly that the Egyptians heard him, and Pharaoh's household heard about it" (Genesis 45:2).

- When revealing himself to his beloved brother Benjamin, Joseph "threw his arms around [him] and wept" (Genesis 45:14).

- When he finally reunited with his father, Joseph "wept for a long time" (Genesis 46:29).

- When his father, Jacob, died, "Joseph threw himself on his father and wept over him" (Genesis 50:1).

- When Joseph's brothers still believed Joseph had not forgiven them, they sent a message asking for forgiveness (again), leading Joseph to weep (Genesis 50:17).

Though it may seem like Joseph's tears were not all connected to grief, I believe that they were. Even in his moments of reconciliation, there was still a deep emotional release—a connection to all that had been lost even with the hope of what was to come. Grief is our human response to what is broken in our world. We were not wired for suffering and pain but for belonging and connection. Tears are our hearts' language, keeping us aware of our vulnerable state as human beings and signaling our deep need for connection.

It's the story of Joseph. It's also the story of Jesus when He walked the earth. Jesus wept deeply as He saw the suffering, pain, and death around Him—whether the death of His friend Lazarus (John 11:35) or

Tears are our hearts' language, keeping us aware of our vulnerable state as human beings and signaling our deep need for connection.

the lost in the city of Jerusalem (Luke 19:41). And then, when He neared the Crucifixion, He poured out His heart to His Father: "During the days of Jesus' life on earth, he offered up prayers and petitions with fervent cries and tears to the one who could save him from death" (Hebrews 5:7).

Tears are also part of our story, and getting through loss can't be worked like a diet program. Its resolution can't be packaged up into a three-step process (to try to do that wouldn't honor the sacredness and the mystery of the kind of fruit that grows only when watered by tears). To emerge from this season with new life, we must honor our tears, face our losses, and allow the great alchemy of God's love to make something beautiful. We need the supportive elements that we have already considered: humility, trust, patience. But I tread lightly into this space because our experience with grief is as unique as our fingerprints. As Richard Exley says in his helpful book *When You Lose Someone You Love*, "In times like these we must always resist the temptation to speak where God has not spoken."[4]

One of the reasons we may struggle with grief is because we've avoided it for so long. We've accumulated losses and we've never known why, how, or when to process them. We sense that grief has power, and we don't know if we'll be able to hold it all together when we consider all that's fallen apart.

Grief can hollow you out or fill you with so much anger you have to find an outlet to simply keep breathing. Grief can numb you to everything around you while simultaneously bringing searing, specific pain when a moment, place, or word sparks a memory. Grief can be like trying to sleep without covers on a cold, damp night or like a freezing wind blasting through an open window when you least expect it. Its jagged path of destruction looks different for each of us. Grief takes an enormous amount of energy, but you can't "work it" until it's gone. There are ways to help alleviate grief—but they can never completely remove it. When you experience a loss, it is yours forever. And the more you loved, the more painful the loss, whether that loss was an actual death or a spiritual or emotional loss. It could be the loss of a job, a friendship, a way of life, a location. Anytime something we love is no longer there for us, whether a person, place, or thing, we experience the human mystery of grief.

New Life after Loss

But from what grief destroys, new things can grow. The destruction can yield new creation, but not without leaving indelible marks on our hearts.

So my hope in this space is to simply allow you room to lean into the tears and the questions, trusting that God has good intentions for you. If God is for you and me, then He is with us. And if He is with, we have the security of His presence. And given His presence with us and His posture *for* us, we can know He is for us. That means . . .

> We can be honest.
> We can take comfort.
> We can state our case.
> We can rest our case.

If God is for us . . . we can be honest

If God's presence is with us and He is for us, we can stop pretending we are okay. We don't have to hold it together for God. We don't have to reframe our pain into purpose or spin our failure into success. We don't have to be anything but who we really are, whether we are bewildered, furious, or crushed. We are permitted to be honest about where we are in the story and to allow many different things to be true at one time. We can be frustrated that God isn't giving us answers while also desperately needing His comfort. We can be so crushed by our grief that we don't want to go on while also asking God to give us the strength to show up for another day. We can be deeply discouraged while also grateful for the small comforts and kindnesses we receive.

Honesty is simply finding ourselves where we are today, in this moment, and opening up our hearts to share that with God. If God is for us, then we don't even have to know what to do with where we are. We don't have to be able to tell God how we are really doing or tell Him where we want to be. We can invite the Spirit to intercede for us, groaning with words that we ourselves cannot express (Romans 8:26).

Not long ago, our daughter, Cameron, was injured in a freak accident. While playing for her school's field hockey team, she was hit with a ball at very close range, resulting in a painful and traumatic injury to her face, mouth, and teeth that required emergency care. Throughout the long night in the ER as we waited for her to be seen, I sat listening to her whimper quietly with her head on my shoulder. Meanwhile I rehearsed every worst-case scenario of what might happen to her. I felt completely helpless without words, requests, or anything to say to the Lord. All I could do was silently whisper *Help* over and over again. I did not have the background to know what treatment or doctor to ask God to send. I did not have the power or control to make anything happen in that waiting room as the hours ticked by. I certainly didn't have the emotional fortitude to keep reassuring Cameron, over and over, as she held a towel to her bleeding face and asked me why we couldn't get help.

The only thing I had was the promise that I've come to believe: In our darkest moments, the Spirit is interceding for us, even when we cannot intercede for ourselves. By 2 a.m., Cameron was stitched up, and thankfully, this injury was a minor blip in her story. Still, before help arrived, as the clock ticked along in the emergency room, nothing held my attention but her pain and my powerlessness to fix it. I could not work any kind of plan to engage with God. I couldn't do the "right" thing to get what I wanted. The only way I could engage with God was through honesty, and honesty meant merely calling *Help.*

If God is for us, we can be honest. We can ask our questions or ask nothing at all. We can be angry, sad, tired, or tired of being angry or sad, and we can simply share that with Him.

The hardest time in my own unexpected season was always the morning, when my eyes opened to the reality that I was still in a hard place, that my next steps were still unresolved, that I was still sad. I knew David's prayer in Psalm 143:8—"Let the morning bring me word of your unfailing love"—but with grief welling up inside me, I did not feel God's unfailing love. What I usually felt was panic, anger, or a settled dread that things were no different from how I had left them before drifting into sleep.

Knowing that I could be honest with God and allow my prayer to be a simple request for His love shifted my perspective. When my eyes opened each morning, I wanted answers, I wanted justice, I wanted purpose, I wanted the redeemed story. But trusting in the tears meant requesting nothing more for the day than a sign of His love. Trusting the tears meant that I could be sad *and* experience God's kindness. That simple prayer is one that He answered, in a million different little ways, over and over again. Signs of His love came in all kinds of ways: in the Scripture I read in the morning, in a friend's encouraging text. It came in the form of readers sending me an email thanking me for my ministry on the very day I wanted to give up. It came in the form of a sunny day, a hug from one of my teenagers, a seemingly random opportunity to help out another church or pastor. These small moments of confirmation were little lights in the tunnel that beckoned me to keep going for one more day. Trusting in the tears meant I could claim, as Joseph did, that God can make me fruitful even in suffering, *especially* in suffering. No matter how hard it was to feel like it was okay—it still, somehow, was okay.

If God is for us . . . we can take comfort

Another consistent theme of unexpected seasons is that the things that were comfortable are no longer so. Things that we may have taken for granted—health, relationships, jobs, even life—have been lost in some way. We may have worked for years to find people, places, and things that were known and allowed us to be known. They were not perfect, but they were ours, and that settled sense of belonging carried us forward. Only when they are stripped away do we discover what foundation our emotional stability, purpose, and joy were built upon.

Jesus warned His followers about the tendency to build life upon the wrong things by telling a story about two houses (Matthew 7:24-29). They look the same on the outside. It's only when the wind and rain lash down upon those houses that their true strength is revealed. The strength isn't in the building materials, design, or aesthetics; rather, it is based solely on the soil its foundation sits upon. You can build a brick house on sand, but no matter how firm the brick and how solid the design, it will slide in a storm. We know this, we believe it, but what's mysterious about life is how easy it is to build dwelling places for our souls on shaky ground.

We may have claimed allegiance to Christ and desire to build upon His foundation, but then we get caught up in building other things, good things—our vocations, budgets, friend groups. We build hobbies and we build our marriages and our children. We build our opinions, our rhythms, and our churches, and all the while, our dependence on these "side projects" becomes the actual foundation of our identity and hope. And it's only when one of them slides off its foundation that we may discover the sense that our whole world is sliding away from us with it. This is not to say that building things in life is futile or foolish—nor are we called to guard our hearts in such a way that we won't feel pain and suffering in our unexpected seasons. However, when we trust the new growth that can come from our grief, we discover in our desperation that even when all else fails, God never will.

How do we receive the comfort of God? We do so by first claiming what is true: "God is our merciful Father and the source of all comfort" (2 Corinthians 1:3, NLT). That means that whatever you've lost was never the source of comfort in the first place—it was something used by God or by you to give you comfort. That person, place, or thing may be gone, but the source of comfort never fails, is always available, and never runs out. The actual source has always been your merciful Father.

Second, we understand that mourning comes before receiving comfort. "God blesses those who mourn, for they will be comforted" (Matthew 5:4, NLT). When we mourn, we honestly acknowledge what has been lost—no spin, no reframing, no fixing, no blaming. Mourning with God is an act of faith. It's believing that His comfort will come, even when we have no answers. It's trusting that even in our darkness, God has not abandoned us. It's surrendering to His goodness even when everything feels bad.

Third, we acknowledge that the Father gives us "eternal comfort and a wonderful hope" (2 Thessalonians 2:16, NLT). We realize that some situations may never be fixed the way we want them to be. Some trials are permanent; some decisions change our lives irrevocably. But to acknowledge our eternal comfort is to return to the very source of the spring of life. It is to walk back from the destruction of what we might be experiencing, to walk upstream, to be reminded that what has been destroyed or removed is a temporal reality. This is why I love the practice of journaling. Many times in life, I've flipped back through old journals to find signs of God's faithfulness—and the signs are always there.

If you haven't kept a journal before, now is a good time to start. God's people are made to remember. And if you don't yet have your own journal of remembering, you can look to the Bible, which is a journal of remembering for all of us. The psalmists consistently remember as a way to find comfort in distress. The stories of God's people are our stories. The God of miracles and resurrection power, the God of hope and second chances, the God of mercy and forgiveness—that's our God, our source of eternal comfort.

Our souls were not designed for death—they were designed for life, and they were made to live forever. Our souls reject death because we weren't made for it. Our souls were also not designed for the pain or destruction that comes into our lives through circumstances or sin, whether our own or others. When we seek this eternal hope, then, it must go beyond the temporal. We go to the only source that can comfort and quench our thirst for life, justice, purpose, and presence. As the promise of blessing continues from the line of Abraham, Isaac, Jacob, and Joseph, it culminates in Christ, who renames blessing as our ability to "have streams of living water flow" *through* us (John 7:38, CSB). Once again, we remember that blessing is never just for us—it's through us. And the very place of our brokenness and grief, as well as our tears, can become a spring of strength that begins with the comfort of Christ and flows out from us to our world.

In a strange paradox, it is often through our own vulnerability and pain that our compassion for others can grow exponentially. And our compassion is the true source of our love.

Compassion asks us to go where it hurts, to enter into places of pain, to share in brokenness, fear, confusion, and anguish. Compassion challenges us to cry out with those in misery, to mourn with those who are lonely, to weep with those in tears. Compassion requires us to be weak with the weak, vulnerable with the vulnerable, and powerless with the powerless. Compassion means full immersion in the condition of being human.[5]

I have a visceral memory of entering a cafeteria where I knew not a single soul. It was the middle of eighth grade and my first day at a new school in a new state. The memory is seared into my heart like a tattoo: standing by myself, gripping my lunch bag against my chest like a shield, looking out at table after table of teenagers, hoping that someone might look up and catch my eye, that someone might scoot over and make room for me, that someone would *see* my painful circumstances and respond. I can pinpoint this moment in eighth grade as the exact moment of pain that God has used in my life to this day—a deep compassion for those who feel like they don't belong or don't have a seat at the table. God used that compassion (quite literally) when I volunteered as a middle school youth leader; He used it in my work later as a therapist; He continues to use it in the way I teach the Bible, in the way I hug my kids' friends, in my desire for justice and equity in my city. Compassion is often born out of pain, yet it is also the fertile ground where purpose becomes fruitful, sometimes ten times, twenty times, one hundred times more fruitful than the suffering. This is not because God loves suffering—but it is because, in His ways that we cannot fully understand, He uses that suffering for the greatest redemptive good.

> Compassion is often born out of pain, yet it is also the fertile ground where purpose becomes fruitful, sometimes ten times, twenty times, one hundred times more fruitful than the suffering.

Because God is for us, we can take comfort. And that comfort becomes the source of our greatest gift to others: the ability to offer them the living stream of comfort through our compassion.

If God is for us . . . we can state our case

Right now you may be confused, angry, exhausted, sad. You may
have times when you feel helpless and wordless, but also times
when you feel angry and full of evidence to justify your grief.
All of this is valuable. All of it is important. Your pain needs an
outlet, and your uncertainty needs resolution. If you do not take
your case to God, you will find yourself seeking justice on your
own terms. You will prosecute people who've wronged you. You'll
prosecute yourself. You will seek to blame someone or something, and that cycle of prosecution and blame is not the direction of redemption or healing. However, it's often a necessary
cycle in order to truly get to the source of your grief: "Though
he slay me, yet will I hope in him; I will surely defend my ways
to his face" (Job 13:15).

The prophet Jeremiah is often known as the "weeping
prophet." His writings reveal this push and pull of grief with
God—coming to God with his arguments about his suffering,
his work, and his circumstances. After being arrested, beaten,
and put in stocks by the priest for prophesying, Jeremiah com-
plains to God: "You deceived me" (Jeremiah 20:7). He wrestles
with God about the ongoing pain of being persecuted for
preaching and living out the truth. Jeremiah could have phrased
the term, "Darned if I do, darned if I don't." If I obey God,
I suffer. If I don't obey God, I cannot hold His words inside
of me (verse 9). In verse 12, Jeremiah is ready to rest his case
with God. But by verse 14, he shouts, "Cursed be the day I was
born!"

Apparently, God is just fine with us making our arguments.
God is patient as we process. God is willing to allow us to state our
case, as many times as we need. And God is also ready to receive
us as we run out of steam, as we run out of questions, and as we
rest our case with Him.

If God is for us . . . we can rest our case

When the words run out, when we have circled the same questions over and over, when we've allowed ourselves to express our grief, when we cannot resolve any more questions, we are on the threshold of release. To release is to rest our case before our merciful and righteous Judge. It's to believe the antinomy that God will take account of all wrongs "before the judgment seat of Christ" (2 Corinthians 5:10) *and* that "as far as the east is from the west, so far has [God] removed our transgressions from us" (Psalm 103:12). Somehow in God's economy, He can reconcile justice and mercy. Somehow He can offer forgiveness but also hold the wicked accountable. To release is to rest our case, knowing that God is somehow able to do something with our pain that we can't even imagine in this season—that He actually can do something transformative, beautiful, and pure with what feels like death.

We may not be able to rest our case for long—we may, like the prophet Jeremiah, be ruing the day we were born just a few moments later—but if God is for us *and* God is our merciful and righteous Judge, we can state our case and rest that case with Him. That's how it happened for Jeremiah. Despite the suffering, despite what he could not understand, he was still able to write in Lamentations: "Because of the Lord's great love we are not consumed, for his compassions never fail. They are new every morning; great is your faithfulness" (Lamentations 3:22-23). That's how it happened for Joseph, who we know was able to say at the end of the story, "You intended to harm me, but God intended it for good" (Genesis 50:20). And that's how it happened for Jesus, who knew what it was to enter into the suffering of the human condition, who wept deeply, who even asked his Father if there was another way besides the Cross.[6] Jesus pleaded and then rested His case with the Father. We need no other example to understand how God invites our honesty and offers His comfort—even when we do not understand why He is allowing our pain.

When we rest our case with God, we can then rest with Him and in Him. We can rest with what's not known and not good, believing that He does know and He is good, and that the only place of true comfort is our God. He is the source of our strength, healing, and resurrection through even the worst valley of death. "I rest my case with you" (Jeremiah 20:12, MSG).

Practices of Lament

Just as our grief is as unique as each one of us, our practices of grief will be too. What works for one might be exhausting for another. Because grief leaves us empty, there is often a sense that there's not much to work with. What do I do with regret or a desire to turn back time? What do I do with imaginary conversations that will never be had; crossroads in the past where I should have taken a different turn; questions about why now, why this, why me? As opposed to seasons of deconstruction, times when we may take apart portions of our faith or vocation in order to renovate, grief is a season of destruction. Renovation won't work in destruction. Only creation is possible after destruction. And if that's true, then it's reasonable to expect that practices of creation are also places of healing and strength in times of grief.

I asked you recently on social media about your practices for lament and grief, and a few of you talked about gardening. You shared your love of getting your hands in the dirt, of the grounded practice of weeding, watering, waiting. Allowing yourself to focus on slow growth and beauty may inspire you to release what was in order to embrace what's coming, and yanking out weeds is a wonderfully vicarious way to express the anger, frustration, and disappointment you hold about what's been lost. Others shared with me your practice of baking, finding comfort in combining simple ingredients that transform into nourishment and comfort. In his book *The Inner Voice of Love*, Henri Nouwen shares the journal entries he wrote during his own unexpected season of anguish and brokenness: "Writing became part of my struggle for survival. It gave me the little distance from myself that I needed to keep from drowning in my despair."[7] Journaling allowed him to slowly heal.

I also have learned that such tactical practices are necessary to make space for grief. Allowing sadness to be a part of the story and welcoming tears as the muddy trail to deeper revelation of my own insecurity, fear, and pain allowed the darkness to slowly, almost imperceptibly lift. As tired as I was of crying, as emotionally taxing as it was for my go-getter, keep-moving personality to do nothing but release the emotion and rest my case, there was no other way. Grief is as deep as the love that you lost. Grief requires so much because you felt so much, you invested so much, you loved so much. In some ways, to honor the slow process of grief is to honor yourself for the way you invested, committed, loved. And slowly, slowly, often in circles, you will move from the darkest night to the long gray dawn that promises that someday soon, the light will shine again.

Do not deny the tears. Do not rush the grief. I know you are tired of feeling sad, bruised, crushed. But it is only in the tears that you will find the truth. It is only when all else fails that you are fully open to the comfort of Christ. Accepting the tears will also allow you to recognize the beauty of the life you have even right now in the darkness. Resting your case does not deny the pain or lessen the grief. But acceptance allows you to see the goodness that still surrounds you.

Acceptance is Joseph naming his children Manasseh and Ephraim. Acceptance is letting God write the story even without the ending you want. Acceptance is believing in God's dream for you even when it appears that dream is drastically different from what you expected and hoped for.

For when we trust, we rest.

A PRAYER FOR WHEN YOU ARE READY TO REST

Well, God,

I claim that I've staked my life on Your promises,
but I keep forgetting to believe them.
It's easier to find a million ways to fix it,
to self-care and self-cope
and self-protect
until I'm exhausted and brittle with the effort.
So, Lord, for the millionth time,
I surrender again.
I rest my case with You.
I give up on getting it right and give in to
    Your grace.
Help me rest here a little while.
And thanks in advance—
we both know I'll be here again.

Amen, anyway.

PART 3

TRIUMPH

Don't believe in kings; believe in the Kingdom.

CHANCE THE RAPPER

Now Joseph was the governor of the land, the person who sold grain to all its people. So when Joseph's brothers arrived, they bowed down to him with their faces to the ground. As soon as Joseph saw his brothers, he recognized them, but he pretended to be a stranger and spoke harshly to them. "Where do you come from?" he asked.

"From the land of Canaan," they replied, "to buy food."

Although Joseph recognized his brothers, they did not recognize him. Then he remembered his dreams about them and said to them, "You are spies! You have come to see where our land is unprotected."

"No, my lord," they answered. "Your servants have come to buy food. We are all the sons of one man. Your servants are honest men, not spies."

GENESIS 42:6-11

CHAPTER 9

GLIMMERS OF REDEMPTION

Now there is a final reason I think that Jesus says, "Love your
enemies." It is this: that love has within it a redemptive power.
And there is a power there that eventually transforms individuals.

MARTIN LUTHER KING JR.

Like Martin Luther King Jr., I believe in love's redemptive power.
Love is the only force with more power than pain. But pain is
a force too. Pain has the unique power to make our lives either
smaller or bigger. If we keep resisting the love and letting the pain
fester and eat at us, we will find ourselves growing older but not
wiser. We've all known people like this—people who let the past
define them, who seem to become more bitter and despairing as
time goes on. The pain might be from something that's happened
to them or something they've done. Most likely, it's a little bit of
both.

Why do some people seem to shine ever more brightly through
the difficulties in life while others seem hopelessly broken? I think
the apostle Paul provides an answer when he writes, "When I was
a child, I talked like a child, I thought like a child, I reasoned like
a child. When I became a man, I put the ways of childhood behind

me" (1 Corinthians 13:11). Not everyone takes the journey of growing up, spiritually speaking. Becoming a man (or woman) in the spiritual sense requires squarely facing the pain and disappointments of life while letting love in. It's talking back to the voices of anger, shame, and fear that want us to believe that it will always be this way and that we are not worth loving again. The great gift of our unexpected seasons is the opportunity to let what's painful and difficult become painful and redemptive, that third way of spiritual maturity that allowed Paul to write: "I have learned the secret of being content in any and every situation" (Philippians 4:12).

Redemption is what happens when the heavy weight of our pain is lightened and lifted by love. It's a glimmer of hope even in the darkest of moments. It's a sense of acceptance, connection, or peace even when all seems to be going wrong. It never undoes the past, but it does give us hope for the future. It's the choice to allow God to take the pain, the unknown, and the difficult and to make it into something usable in His hands. Redemption requires both truth and grace, both justice and forgiveness.

Most of us imagine redemption as a linear process: *I lost this but gained back this similar thing; I suffered with this but then got it all back; I was abandoned by this person and the very same person now has sought me out.* However, redemption is neither instantaneous nor transactional. It's not like redeeming a coupon and getting a little cash back. Redemption is a process. It's the result of big and little decisions made over time. The redemption God offers comes on His own terms. It may or may not look like a tidy ending. More likely, it's like a piece of art, an abstract painting that comes together as we allow the great Creator to make masterpieces of our lives. Growing up, spiritually speaking, involves repentance just as much as redemption. The Greek word translated *repent* essentially means "to change one's mind." In the New Testament, that repentance is a change of mind, a moral reorientation toward God.[1] It is the love of God that reveals redemption in our stories, and it is also the love of God that uses all the materials of life to help us leave our childish ways behind, to grow up into His love, to change our minds toward God in repentance.

I've spent my adult life listening to stories. In my student ministry days, I heard stories from teenagers struggling with breakups or struggling with depression, seeking real love and seeking God. As a therapist, I've heard stories of people getting stuck, moving through pain, trying to find the way to beauty even when it seems God has handed them a mess. As a pastor, I've heard stories that are often just as messy but that come with an extra measure of spiritual bewilderment: *I thought I was doing the right thing, but this is not what I signed up for.* And yet repeatedly and consistently, those who face the pain, who hang on to God, who are frustrated with Him and sometimes furious but *faithful anyway* come through their unexpected season saying, "Now I know what it means to trust God." They change their minds about the lie that God has abandoned or forgotten them, or that He is punishing them, and they realize He was there all along, layering light into the shadow of their lives, creating beautiful works of art.

Redemption and Repentance: The Reunion of the Brothers

Our redemption is not linear but multifaceted because we never experience pain in a vacuum. There are always others experiencing our unexpected seasons with us, whether close by or from a distance. And the benefits of redemption are far-reaching, although sometimes challenging to recognize. Let's look at the ways redemption begins to glimmer—not just in Joseph's life, but in his father's and brothers' lives too. As we enter more deeply into Joseph's story, we are invited to turn the narrative, like a diamond, and see it glitter from a different facet.

It had been almost a decade since the night of Pharaoh's dream and the day of Joseph's deliverance. How the tide had turned for Joseph! Becoming the great steward of Egypt, taking a wife, having the boys. Naming and accepting his place in Egypt, living like he belonged there—in his language, dress, and customs. Using all the leadership experience he gained from Potiphar and in prison to faithfully lead Egypt through years of abundance, with that famine always on his mind. And on his mind it was! When the fields were fertile and the people happy, Joseph methodically planned, prepared, adjusted, and managed. Yet all the while he held on to his knowledge of the true God, the God of his fathers.

When everyone was comfortable with plenty, the season of want arrived, just as Pharaoh's dream had foretold. At first "there was famine in all the other lands, but in the whole land of Egypt there was food" (Genesis 41:54). But eventually the famine arrived even in the land of abundance, and when the people of Egypt cried out, Joseph responded. He opened the storehouses and sold grain to the Egyptians, and then eventually "all the world came to Egypt to buy grain from Joseph" (verse 57). I imagine that after giving glory to God, Joseph was gratified to be able to pass this blessing along to the people. How fulfilling it must have been to see his plan come together as people from other lands began to line up to receive food from Egypt's storehouses. Even in the midst of his sorrow and suffering, Joseph saw that God had been faithful. He had shown Joseph the future for Pharaoh, and even though Joseph's own dream hadn't yet been realized, God showed up. God showed mercy, and through the work of Joseph's hands, the people were fed.

And just when the story of Joseph's life seemed settled, just when the glimmers of God's redemptive goodness showed up in Joseph's own children and his meaningful work—his brothers came to Egypt.

When Redemption Looks like Repentance

All along our journey through Genesis, we've experienced what redemption looks like in unexpected suffering. Joseph has been our guide through tests of loss, integrity, and humility. We've seen

Joseph choose God's way repeatedly, giving Him glory from the prison to the palace. But redemption isn't just experienced when or because we do the right thing. Redemption also shows up in repentance: when we recognize the ways we've gone wrong and areas in our lives in which patterns of sin have stained our story. Most of us can relate to "Joseph moments" in our lives, but the reality is that we probably don't experience *only* such moments. When we turn the story to view it from another perspective, that of Joseph's brothers, we see the facet of redemption at work in their lives, too, as the burden of guilt they've carried for years slowly comes to light. This confirms a truth we've likely all experienced: When we keep our pain in the dark, when we refuse to acknowledge our own failures, nothing is healed. In our unexpected seasons, we can be wounded *and* we can wound. We can be disappointed *and* we can disappoint. We may need to forgive *and* we need to be forgiven. This is why redemption can include a painful dose of reality: It enables us to see ourselves for who we truly are and shows us the need to repent of our own sin.

And here's what's beautiful about the redemption available in our failings and doubts: We are reminded that none of us are beyond God's reach. Joseph is an example of moral courage and faithful integrity, but many (if not most) characters in Scripture radically fail—and God's redemptive purposes still extend to them. Resist the urge to believe that if you had been better, stronger, or read your Bible more, you wouldn't be in this season. That wasn't true for Joseph, who had trouble beyond measure. It wasn't true for Jesus, who lived a sinless life but was still misunderstood, mischaracterized, and slandered from the very first year of His ministry. We've already reviewed a few lowlights from the guys in Genesis: Abraham pretended that his wife, Sarah, was his sister to protect himself; Isaac was passive; Jacob was devious. Read a little further, and you'll discover that Moses was angry, Rahab was a prostitute, King David was a murderer. Solomon had an existential crisis, Gideon was scared, and Naomi was bitter. The list could go on and on, and those names are just from the Old Testament.

I've wasted buckets of tears and miles of energy trying to figure out the why of my own unexpected season, but that doesn't seem to be what God's interested in talking about. It's not about what we've done wrong or right in the past; it's about what we are doing in the present. Unexpected seasons are often about seeking God's comfort in the midst of loss and disappointment, but they are also opportunities to grow, to leave behind any ways of believing, acting, or feeling that pull us away from the truth of God's love for us and His sovereignty over all.

God's redemptive work is not dependent on our moral courage or virtue. But our moral courage and virtue are the fruit of God's redemptive work. Just as forgiveness is a process that starts with a willful choice, redemption is a process that starts with surrender and trust. It's one of the best gifts of our salvation. It's God's great plan for our lives, in which He takes what's been painful, lost, or broken and transforms it. God calls this beautiful truth His ability to "give . . . beauty for ashes" (Isaiah 61:3, NLT). When we surrender to God the dreams we've had to let die, the relationships that seem broken beyond repair, the disappointments that haven't resolved, He takes the ashes of our mourning and loss and makes something beautiful. The way He redeems our pain is the most miraculous sign of His love in our everyday lives, and it's available to us all.

> God's redemptive work is not dependent on our moral courage or virtue. But our moral courage and virtue are the fruit of God's redemptive work.

Regardless of what brought about your unexpected season, God is still at work, God is still a redeemer, and God will always be the source of transformation—from pain to purpose. As you hold your own story out for God's healing presence, let's see how the healing light of reality shone for Joseph's brothers.

The Reunion

*Although Joseph recognized his brothers, they did not
recognize him. Then he remembered his dreams about them
and said to them, "You are spies! You have come to see where
our land is unprotected."*

*"No, my lord," they answered. "Your servants have come
to buy food. We are all the sons of one man. Your servants are
honest men, not spies."*

GENESIS 42:8-11

Just as Joseph's character had been revealed over time and through
testing, we now see Joseph engaging in a strategic and intentional
testing of his brothers, which was designed to reveal how they had
grown (or not) since they betrayed him and left him for dead. His
deliberate and drawn-out testing offers a window into how life had
shaped the men over the decades they had been apart. Although we
have the benefit of knowing the end of the story, when the brothers and Joseph met face-to-face, they certainly had no idea how
it would turn out. Joseph knew nothing of the trajectory of his
brothers' lives after their wickedness toward him. And the brothers had no idea what had happened to Joseph, who was as good as
dead to them. It is only through the friction Joseph created that we
get a better sense of exactly who each person had become and how
this story would end. Perhaps this series of tests was Joseph's way of
determining whether it was safe to reveal himself to his brothers,
or if restoration was even possible.

After Joseph accused his brothers of being spies, the men
declared that they were "honest men" (Genesis 42:11). If I were
Joseph, I would wonder, *But are you?* He had experienced the
very worst of who his brothers could be, but who were they now?
As Joseph deliberately hid his own identity and let time pass,
he learned more about exactly what had been going on in his

family during all their years of separation. The "honest men" then shared a little bit of backstory: "Your servants were twelve brothers. . . . The youngest is now with our father, and one is no more" (Genesis 42:13).

Joseph now had one new piece of information: The family was still intact. His beloved younger brother, Benjamin, was alive and well. Joseph then detained this delegation of brothers for three days before commanding that the "youngest brother" be brought back to Egypt as a way to verify their story (Genesis 42:20). At this point, the brothers talked in Hebrew among themselves, not realizing that Joseph could understand them. "Surely we are being punished because of our brother," they said. "We saw how distressed he was when he pleaded with us for his life, but we would not listen; that's why this distress has come on us" (Genesis 42:21).

At this, Joseph had to turn away because he began to weep. Imagine what it must have felt like to know that your brothers, after all these years, remembered the story of your betrayal as if it were yesterday. Imagine the sorrow mixed with vindication as Joseph saw the weight of their own guilt revealed as they squabbled and blamed each other. When Joseph released all his brothers but Simeon so they could journey home, he added one more test. He had the money they were using to buy food from Egypt secretly returned to each of their sacks. When the brothers stopped for the night, one of them—who isn't identified—opened his bag. He saw the silver there and knew it looked like he had stolen—from the *governor of Egypt*! This strange situation orchestrated by Joseph was the final straw, the one that broke their illusion that they were "honest men." Their guilt had caught up to them, and they turned to one another as "their hearts sank" and asked, "What is this that God has done to us?" (Genesis 42:28).

Their hearts sank. Just a few days before, they had declared, "We are honest men!" But over the past hours, they had come face-to-face with who they really were and who they'd been. Their hearts—the centers of their emotional reasoning and souls—fell.

What Joseph had experienced for years, they experienced for days. Joseph had endured painful and long tests of his character that revealed his integrity. The brothers endured tests over a few days that revealed their sin. These examinations brought about a quickening in their consciences that revealed the burden they'd been carrying for years.

And here's the crazy thing about God's redemptive plan: This painful reckoning was *good.* Before a wound can heal, it has to be cleaned out. Our unexpected seasons often bring pain, not only for what's happened to us but also for the ways we've sinned. In God's fierce kindness, He uses tests to reveal our need for both healing and repentance.

A Word on Repentance and Reconciliation

As we take a front-row seat to watch the relationship between Joseph and his brothers play out, we encounter the question that often comes out of our own broken relationships: *What does it look like to love this person now?* Many Christians have been hurt because they believe that forgiving someone and restoring the relationship are the same thing. In our desire to be obedient to the command that we forgive, many of us absorb the idea that regardless of the wound inflicted on us, we should continue to have a relationship with the offender. This is why I love diving deep into the story of Joseph, who is set up as a model of integrity for us but does not blindly rush back into a relationship with his brothers! With Joseph as our guide, we see that although forgiveness can be offered fully, regardless of the response, restoration and reconciliation require both parties to respond, and that's not guaranteed.

Those who've walked through an unexpected season of relational strife, brokenness, or trauma know that the idea of "forgiving and forgetting" is a myth. We can forgive and heal; we can forgive and release; we can forgive and embrace the redemptive story; but forgiveness does not mean a relationship should (or will) be restored. Forgiveness and restoration are two separate experiences. When we've been wounded, whether that wound is the abrupt ending of a friendship or something as traumatic as sexual or physical abuse, we experience the result of sin in the world. Sin is not just about our individual behaviors—although our individual choices can be sinful. Sin is the source of the full fracturing in the world we all live in. Sin causes pain, strife, violence, and darkness on every level—in our nation, in our communities, in our families, and in our hearts. Before sin, there was no death or loss. We weren't designed for either one, so our souls are not equipped for them. We protest against them—as we should. We learn to skip and stuff or dive and dwell; but the real way forward is the redeemed way, and that starts with acknowledging how *wrong* loss and death feel.

A friend of mine taught me the power of grieving what's wrong about loss simply by acknowledging it. I once poured out my heart to him about the confusion and pain I felt over some broken relationships and an uncertain future. As I love to do, I rushed through the painful parts and tried to rationalize what was good in life (*skip and stuff, anyone?*), but before I could get very far, he stopped me and said, "I want you to know that I think what happened to you was wrong, and I am really sad that it did." This is the real and redeemed way—entering fully into what feels hard and broken about it all, but then letting the pain lead us into redemption—into surrender, into deeper trust in God, into wisdom.

Contrary to the fracture of sin is the gift of life. The life Jesus offers is full of healing, joy, and peace. This is precisely why the Good News of Jesus is about much more than your individual sins. Jesus didn't die on the cross just because you ran a red light last month or talked badly about your mother-in-law. Jesus offered His life because the heart of the gospel is wholeness, abundance, and peace—the very things that sin destroys. The work of the gospel is reconciling us back to this truth. Reconciliation brings together what sin has broken apart. The most important reconciliation that can happen in our lives is being reconciled to God through Christ: "In him all the fullness of God was pleased to dwell, and through him to reconcile to himself all things, whether on earth or in heaven, making peace by the blood of his cross" (Colossians 1:19-20, ESV). All reconciliation in our lives flows out of this relationship with Christ. It is through Him that we have "streams of living water" (John 7:38, CSB)—including the ongoing process of forgiveness and redemption throughout our earthly lives. This is why redemption includes repentance. Life is about a continual reconciling of our hearts to God through Jesus Christ. It's this great force of love that's bigger than our pain and that allows us to fail, to sin, to not be perfect, and yet to still be loved, accepted, and forgiven.

Through Christ we are reconciled, and in Christ we are called to be agents of reconciliation in the world. We reconcile as a way of living. As believers, we are called to seek out brokenness in ourselves, in our relationships, and in our society, and then we are called to do the repair work of bringing grace and forgiveness to those places. We see Joseph doing this with his brothers, but it's a process. His strange tests weren't designed to punish the brothers but to allow time and friction to reveal their true selves, not the "honest men" they believed themselves to be. Forgiveness is just what we do when we've been forgiven. But restoration of relationship and trust are processes that take time and transformation from *both* parties.

Joseph didn't reveal himself immediately, and that allowed light to expose the broken places of sin and regret in his brothers. When we shine light on broken places, the people involved may or may not actually decide to join us in the light. When we seek true reconciliation, the people who've hurt us may or may not be willing to repent. Just because we pursue restoration does not mean that those we approach will respond.[2]

Joseph proceeded shrewdly when it came to his brothers, the

very people who'd thrown his life away many years before. Sin corrupts our hearts, our moral conscience, and our understanding of right and wrong. But to His glorious praise, our Creator is patient with us. He is willing to bring what was in the dark into the light for the purposes of redemption and healing—if we will respond. He demonstrates a patient but persistent desire for everyone—sinners, saints, and everyone in between—to come to repentance. And this is how gracious our God is—so loving that He will not impose His will upon us. In His great love, He gives us the freedom to decide whether to respond to His invitation. As C. S. Lewis aptly summarized: "There are only two kinds of people in the end: those who say to God, 'Thy will be done,' and those to whom God says, in the end, '*Thy* will be done.'"[3]

So when we look at Joseph's engagement with his brothers through the lens of God's redemptive plan, we see God sovereignly directing and bringing truth to light. Let's see what happens when everyone impacted by Joseph's disappearance has the opportunity to display moral courage, integrity, and repentance.

Back to the Story: "Everything Is against Me"

After finding the one bag of silver in the sack, the brothers continued the journey back to their father. Once home, they recounted to him their strange experience with the ruler of Egypt. Of course, they left out the part about being overcome with guilt about Joseph's demise (remember, Jacob was led to believe Joseph had been eaten by a wild animal all those years ago). Simeon had been left behind in Egypt, held as collateral until the brothers returned with Benjamin as Joseph commanded. After telling Jacob about their encounter with the Egyptian steward, the brothers opened their bags and discovered that *all* the silver meant as payment for their grain had been returned to each sack! Jacob then revealed his own deep belief about the pain he carried: "You have deprived me of my children. Joseph is no more and Simeon is no more,

and now you want to take Benjamin. *Everything is against me!*"
(Genesis 42:36, emphasis added).

When I led a team of deacons at my former church, one of
our primary functions was to care for people inside and outside
the church who came to us for financial support. In the process
of learning their stories and determining their needs, the deacons
would be uncomfortable entering into the tangled stories that had
brought people to this point. One of our leadership axioms in
those situations was this: "Sometimes you are the sugar, sometimes
the sandpaper." Sometimes mercy looks like sugar, providing the
sweetness and comfort we need. But sometimes mercy looks like
sandpaper, creating friction in order to reveal what's underneath
the surface that might be festering, the deeper wound that needs
God's healing hand.

The friction Joseph created with his little money trick revealed
what was under the surface for both the brothers and for Jacob.
Under duress, the brothers revealed the guilt they had been
carrying. Ever since that fateful day when Joseph had been sold
to the traders, the brothers' storyline had been: *God is punishing us.* Under stress, Jacob revealed the old insecurity of his life,
the one he'd operated under since falling in love with Joseph and
Benjamin's mom, Rachel, way back in Laban's fields. That old
storyline: *Everyone and everything is against me.*

The friction that Joseph created brought all of this pain into
the light. It revealed exactly what was being shaped in his brothers in the decades after Joseph disappeared. It also drew a sharp
distinction between the rewards Joseph and his brothers had been
seeking. The theologian Martin Luther put it this way:

> He who seeks nothing other than holiness is the one who
> seeks God himself, and he will find him. He who seeks
> reward, however, and avoids pain, never finds him at all
> and makes reward his God. Whatever it is that makes a
> man do something, that motive is his god.[4]

Even when our motives are impure, however, God is at work in our circumstances. *It's not the circumstances that shape our lives; it's what we do with the circumstances that ultimately determines the peace we find within ourselves and with God.* At the very moment Jacob felt that "everything is against me," God was working out His plan.

"God Has Uncovered Your Servants' Guilt"

Now the brothers were home, and the famine dragged on. As the story continued, Jacob's ongoing grief and insecurity were revealed. Although he initially refused to let his sons go back with Benjamin, once everyone was hungry again, he became desperate to have them secure more food without taking his beloved youngest son with them. The loss of Joseph came rushing back to the forefront of everyone's minds, despite it having happened so many years before. But the desire for reconciliation was contagious, and new heroes emerged in the story. One brother, Reuben, promised to forfeit his own sons if necessary to bring Benjamin back home safely. Another brother, Judah, urged Jacob to let them go, promising to be responsible for Benjamin. Jacob was finally left with no other options. Hungry, bereaved, and miserable, he released them to travel back to Egypt.

When Joseph heard that his brothers had arrived, this time with their youngest brother, he had a feast prepared and came to meet them. After this second journey, Joseph got even more of a picture of what had been going on at home. "How is your aged father? . . . Is he still living?" he asked. Then his gaze turned to Benjamin. "Is this your youngest brother?" (Genesis 43:27, 29). When he learned that his aging father was still well and that his beloved full brother—the only remaining link to his biological mother—had come, Joseph had to leave the room to conceal his uncontrollable weeping.

Once the feast began, Joseph made sure extra food was piled

on Benjamin's plate. The irony of it all was that while the brothers watched their lives unravel—they'd lost the ability to provide for their families because of the famine, they'd grieved their father because they'd been framed for stealing, they'd spoken of their secret sin because they were sure they were being punished—God was actually being very gracious to them. I love this line from the Oswald Chambers devotional classic *My Utmost for His Highest*: "You may often see Jesus Christ wreck a life before He saves it."[5] Sometimes sugar. Sometimes sandpaper.

The next morning, Joseph enacted his third test. Would his brothers continue to serve their own needs, driven by vengeance and jealousy as they had been when Joseph was a teenager? Or was their guilt leading them to follow a righteous trajectory in life? Joseph sent them back home, their bags again stuffed with grain, but this time, he had his steward place his personal silver cup into Benjamin's sack. As you can imagine, stealing the governor of Egypt's cup was a no-no, so the high drama continued.

> "You may often see Jesus Christ wreck a life before He saves it."
>
> *Oswald Chambers*

Joseph gave the brothers a head start and then sent his servants to track them down and shake them up. "Why have you repaid good with evil?" Joseph directed his steward to say (Genesis 44:4). The brothers replied that whoever had the cup would die—and of course, once the bags were opened, the cup was found in Benjamin's sack. But rather than ditch Benjamin to save themselves, the brothers all returned to the palace to throw themselves down before Joseph.

> *"What can we say to my lord?" Judah replied. "What can we say? How can we prove our innocence? God has uncovered your servants' guilt. We are now my lord's slaves—we ourselves and the one who was found to have the cup."*
> GENESIS 44:16

What sorrow and pain Joseph must have felt in this moment as he watched his dream literally come true before his eyes in a way he could have never imagined or desired! And yet in the midst of the pain (Joseph's weeping attests to that), we also have hope. Joseph had continually tested his brothers—*whoever is guilty will be my slave.* And yet Reuben and now Judah continued to step up, to sacrifice, to protect their father at great cost to themselves. Remember—at this point the brothers still had no idea who Joseph was. All they knew was that in a terrible turn of karma, the guilt they'd carried over their brother's demise seemed thrown back in their faces. The very thing they'd done (give evil for good) and the very act of sending their brother into slavery was now the fate they themselves faced.

Bowing down before Joseph, they declared that they were all his slaves. I believe that this moment is the beginning of repentance, as they came clean before Joseph and threw themselves at his mercy. Now Joseph gave them one more test. "Only the man who was found to have the cup will become my slave. The rest of you, go back to your father in peace" (Genesis 44:17). Would the brothers return to their self-protective ways? Would they allow Benjamin to be the sacrificial offering? Would they make up another story about his demise, covering for themselves again like they'd done so many years ago with Joseph? But God's blessings tend to work themselves out in the strangest of ways, and now Judah (the same Judah who grossly mistreated his daughter-in-law in Genesis 38, another story for another day) stepped up. Judah recounted his version of the last few months, allowing Joseph to hear exactly what had been told to his father. Judah shared it all—including Jacob's own words about what had happened to Joseph: "One of [my sons] went away from me, and I said, 'He has surely been torn to pieces.' And I have not seen him since" (verse 28). And in a great reversal from that terrible day when Joseph was separated from his family, Judah now offered his own life in exchange for Benjamin's:

Please let your servant remain here as my lord's slave in place of the boy, and let the boy return with his brothers. How can I go back to my father if the boy is not with me? No! Do not let me see the misery that would come on my father.

GENESIS 44:33-34

Now Joseph knew the whole story. Now Joseph knew that the brothers must have schemed to make his disappearance seem like an accidental death ("He has surely been torn to pieces"). This whole time, his father hadn't known that he had been sold into slavery, didn't know there was a chance Joseph could still be alive. Meanwhile, his brothers had watched their father grieve and mourn, touched deeply by a sadness they could not relieve. And now Judah—treacherous, lecherous, selfish Judah—stood up to the still-unknown Joseph and offered his life in exchange for Benjamin's. The process of redemption had begun, and it started with Judah's second chance to do the right thing. This time, he chose righteousness. Perhaps hearts really do change. Perhaps redemption works itself out in mysterious ways.

Through all the trials, God had not forgotten Joseph. And in the years after Joseph was ripped from all he knew, God had not forgotten his family. It took some sandpaper to bring out what had been covered by so many years of secrets. But in the testing, the true growth of his brothers had been revealed. Where there had been jealousy, resentment, and self-protection, now there was sacrificial love, care for their father, and concern for one another. Tests only reveal what is already there.

And at this point, Joseph had seen everything he needed to see. It was time for the real reunion.

A PRAYER FOR WHEN WE NEED HELP FORGIVING

God of restoration,

Sometimes I confuse forgiveness
with justice.
I tell myself that once You bring things into the light,
once recompense arrives,
once my enemies bow,
I will be the most merciful heart of all . . . but
*   only then.*
But You know me better than that.
You know that I twist vengeance
and call it justice.
I harbor bitterness
and call it truth. . . .
And yet you are a God who forgives even that
*   ugliness in me.*
So will You teach me to forgive these
much smaller matters?
Cheers to grace.

Amen.

Then Joseph could no longer control himself before all his attendants, and he cried out, "Have everyone leave my presence!" So there was no one with Joseph when he made himself known to his brothers. And he wept so loudly that the Egyptians heard him, and Pharaoh's household heard about it.

Joseph said to his brothers, "I am Joseph! Is my father still living?" But his brothers were not able to answer him, because they were terrified at his presence.

Then Joseph said to his brothers, "Come close to me." When they had done so, he said, "I am your brother Joseph, the one you sold into Egypt! And now, do not be distressed and do not be angry with yourselves for selling me here, because it was to save lives that God sent me ahead of you. . . .

"Tell my father about all the honor accorded me in Egypt and about everything you have seen. And bring my father down here quickly."

Then he threw his arms around his brother Benjamin and wept, and Benjamin embraced him, weeping. And he kissed all his brothers and wept over them.

GENESIS 45:1-5, 13-15

CHAPTER 10

REDEMPTION: THE LONG STORY

Not only so, but we also glory in our sufferings,
because we know that suffering produces perseverance;
perseverance, character; and character, hope.

ROMANS 5:3-4

A few years after being diagnosed with cancer in 1977, Bob Marley, the singer who brought reggae to the world, wrote what many call his magnum opus, a simple, truthful, hopeful work of art: "Redemption Song." Since his untimely death at thirty-six, "Redemption Song" has gone on to be featured in several major movies, been covered by artists like Stevie Wonder and Madonna, and brought together Pearl Jam's Eddie Vedder and Beyoncé in a duet. It was even sung by John Legend at the 2017 Nobel Peace Prize ceremony. "Redemption Song" envisions a hopeful future in which we can overcome the oppression and destruction of generations before us. Writer Ian McCann sums up the message of the song this way:

> Your existence is not defined by the world powers, by destructiveness, by evil; your purpose is not dictated to

by the mighty, but by the Almighty. Your heroes may die, you may be oppressed, you may feel you can't prevent the wrong things happening, but the universe is bigger than that. Join this song. You have the power to free your mind and soul. You can be redeemed.[1]

"The universe is bigger than that. Join this song." Isn't that what we all really hope for? If you've moved past anger into acceptance, if you've allowed sadness to comingle with joy, the final curve in your journey is the great question of your heart: *Will God redeem this season? Does God care enough about me to bring something beautiful out of all this brokenness?* You may be tempted to quiet the pleading song of your heart and listen to the doctrine in your head. *Of course, God is redeeming this,* your mind might say. *Here are a few things He's already done in my story . . .* Yes, this recognition is good and necessary, and you probably need these reasons to come to mind as a coping mechanism in the hardest and darkest days. But what I'm asking you to consider goes much deeper. What I'm asking is that you not only intellectually agree with the things of God but that you would allow His character and promises to flow out of your heart. The pleading song of your heart is the place of greatest need and greatest truth. The glory of your unexpected season will be the ability to sing a redemption song, even in the pain.

This is the hope of the gospel, the story of Joseph, the message of this book. The great promise we've been chasing comes down to asking ourselves the most difficult question: *Can God redeem even this?*

Redemption is perhaps the greatest promise, the greatest hope of our humanity. The obsession with redemption isn't limited to Bible stories and reggae songs. It's all around us. Redemption is the great theme in superhero movies and epic novels. Redemption plays out on our sports fields, high school reunions, and even events like fundraiser 5Ks created in response to families' tragedies.

Apparently, the power of redemption is actually good for us. A longitudinal study conducted over fifteen years found that adults who were able to highlight redemptive stories in their own lives had high levels of psychological health, as well as generativity, which is defined as: "a strong commitment to promoting the well-being of future generations and improving the world in which they live."[2] This study would attest to this truth: It's not the exact circumstances of our unexpected seasons that determine if we can sing a redemption song. No matter the trouble, it's how we process and engage with our painful circumstances that matters. The essence of abundant life—our wellness, our wholeness, our connection to greater purpose—is connected to the way we tell the story of redemption.

Redemption, Defined

When it comes to the hard seasons of life, redemption is our ability to allow hard things to be hard while believing they're also being used for good. It's the process of holding together both the truth of our current situation and the hope of our preferred future. Redemption is that third way, the practice of living between skipping and stuffing and dwelling and diving. It's swimming into the deep end of life; the place of truth, meaning, grief, repentance. It's entering into the suffering and believing in the beauty on the other side. In a study of adults living into their redemptive stories, researchers define redemption as enduring "suffering to attain enhancement later on."[3]

The dictionary defines the action of redeeming as:

to free from what distresses or harms: such as
a. to *free* from captivity by payment of ransom
b. to *extricate* from or help to overcome something detrimental
c. to *release* from blame or debt: clear
d. to *free* from the consequences of sin[4]

I want you to think about the particular places in your story where you feel stuck. I want you to think about what's unexpected, unfulfilled, unexplainable. Now take these action phrases and apply them to your situation.

When I think about _____, do I want to be: freed from this mental prison? extricated from something detrimental? released from this burden? freed from the pain of sin? simply . . . freed?

Notice that *redeemed* is not a synonym for *vindicated* or *justified* (unfortunately). So often in my own life, I've confused redemption for revenge, but in the nicest possible way. I want God to set a table before my enemies and then run them through a twenty-two-point sermon on how they've wronged me and why He's mad at them because of it. Of course, I don't want to be the one called into God's presence as the bad guy (as I surely would be), but it would be nice if every wrong could be undone while I'm the beneficiary. But redemption isn't about your enemies groveling as you feast. It's about being so free from the evil done to you that you want your enemies to pull up a chair and feast with you. It's being so free of blame and condemnation toward yourself or anyone else that you can see the good in even the worst of situations.

My friend Gabe says it like this: "When my heart is full of gratitude—for what God has done in my life, for what God has shaped in me—then my posture is of benevolence toward the world. From that place, I can release. I can bless." Redemption is all about the long story—longer even than our unexpected seasons. The work of redemption started before we even knew we'd be in this place and will continue long after this season is behind us. Redemption is like a large tree that grows from a small seed. It's like the kingdom that Jesus came to show us.

Redemption as Art

As we come to the conclusion of Joseph's story, God paints us a picture of what redemption looks like. We must keep in mind that it's a painting, not a prescription. When we read any story, the temptation is to immediately insert our own circumstances and demand that God show up in the same way; or to condemn ourselves as failures or less beloved because our story isn't shaping up with such linear resolution. But to do either is to miss the beauty of the brushstrokes, the nuance of the pen, the unique way that God is shaping our lives and stories.

The blessing, however, is the same:

Do not be afraid.
God is here.
God has plans to accomplish good for you and through you.

In my own story, redemption kept showing up in the redwood forests of California. Two years after serving in Saratoga, I was once again in the near-mythical woods of the Santa Cruz Mountains, leading a women's retreat at Mount Hermon. For the first time, I was teaching the rough-draft version of this content, sharing pieces of my own story while discovering what God had to say to all of us in our unexpected seasons. After my second session, I invited anyone who wanted to join me out on the patio, under the trees, to share what unexpected seasons looked like in their own lives and what redemption song God was writing in them. So many women showed up that we ran out of space, and they opened their hearts wide. Story after story of loss and change: the impact of COVID-19; the burnout of teachers and nurses; death, divorce, illness, job loss. The details were different, but the pain was deep and somehow communal as we made space to share, to both honor the pain and seek the hope of redemption within the stories.

One woman pointed up to the trees. "See these redwoods? Do you know that fire makes them stronger? It's only when there's fire that they release their seeds. Fire is the perfect time for new things to grow."[5] She pointed up at the big trees again, her voice growing louder and more jubilant, "And when I thought about my own life, and these trees, I said 'I don't want to let this fire just burn me. I want to grow!'" She began to laugh and whoop a bit, adding, "Don't let the fire just burn you!" She had survived cancer. She had found her way back to joy. She had earned the right to tell us that we could have hope. As she shared her story, a little ripple of joy coursed through that group of women gathered under the trees.

Redemption is always multifaceted. Our pain can be used for God's purposes, whether in the mighty ways we serve or in the little ways we bring joy to a group of strangers. These are the little and mighty miracles of the redemption songs of our hearts.

That is the promise. The unique circumstances are different. God isn't doing an old thing or a repeated thing or a formulaic thing in you; He's doing a new thing. So even as you see your story come to its resolution, my hope and prayer is that you pay attention to what God is painting in your life right now—the beautiful masterpiece of your own redemption.

Redemption after Acceptance

The conclusion of Joseph's story—what we may assume Joseph perceived as the "end state" dream, with his brothers bowing before him—turned out to be only one brushstroke in his redemption masterpiece. After all, when his brothers threw themselves down in front of him, Joseph didn't choose that moment to reveal himself: "Aha! I got you! It's me, Joseph! Remember when I dreamed this would happen? Ha, ha, *here we are, bros!*"

If anything, Joseph was grieved by his brothers' sorrow and guilt, repeatedly leaving their presence because he was overcome by tears. Seeing his dream come true was merely a wayfinding sign on this trail of redemption, a reminder that God had been with Joseph all along.

The choices we read Joseph making in Genesis 45 weren't due to his brothers' actions as they threw themselves on his mercy; he made these choices despite their actions. He didn't just stumble into reconciliation, as if hearts could change that fast. By the time he revealed himself to his brothers, his story had already been reconciled, his heart already settled, his case already at rest with God.

Redemption, it turns out, is one of the fruits of acceptance. Only when we've surrendered our lives to God's way and recognized that, even in this valley, the Lord has good for us can we open our eyes to our own redemption stories. This looks like acceptance; it looks like repentance; it looks like the practice of giving ourselves over to God's provision each day, giving us enough light to keep going, enough hope to press on.

We all have a choice to make: Will we discover what redemption looks like in our unique situation and then choose to walk in it? Or will we continue to skip and stuff—oblivious to what God wants to do in and through us—or dive and dwell in our sadness, anger, or pain? Choosing the path of redemption is a characteristic of abundant life, true life. Every day, we choose the ways of death or the ways of life. The former are characterized by self-seeking, self-protecting, and self-glorifying choices made to avoid facing our pain, our limitation, our sin, our need for a Savior. The ways of life are characterized by dying to our old patterns and choosing to follow Jesus into an abundant life where we allow our suffering and pain to be redeemed for His glory.

Choosing life is one of the key exhortations in Scripture.

- Joseph's story is full of allusions to choices that led to death or life. In his final reveal to his brothers, he asserted that all his suffering had happened "for . . . the saving of many lives" (Genesis 50:20).

- Moses exhorted the Israelite people to choose to follow God's way: "I have set before you life and death, blessings and curses. Now choose life" (Deuteronomy 30:19).

- Proverbs contains this wisdom: "The fruit of the righteous is a tree of life, and the one who is wise saves lives" (Proverbs 11:30).

- Jesus tells us: "I have come that [you] may have life" (John 10:10).

Jesus is referring not simply to our physical life (although we are sustained through His powerful word every day, according to Hebrews 1:3). Instead He offers us a life in which we have the choice to live fully, deeply, and joyfully in even the most unexpected, unexplainable, and uncertain circumstances. This is our redemption song, connected to something much bigger than our pain in the moment. The story of Joseph is unique, just like our stories. It's human and it's hard and it's long. God was mostly silent, but He was certainly not absent.

God may be mostly silent in your story, but He is certainly not absent.

Joseph's dream was unfolding before his eyes; yet it was full of the brothers' guilt and fear, Joseph's sadness, Jacob's grief, and a million other hard things no one would choose. And yet. And yet God was still at work. This story would have ramifications for generations to come—rippling through history even to this very moment for me and you.

So let's get back to the story as the narrative of the guilt-stricken brothers, a grief-stricken father, and the long-lost dreamer intersect.

And Now . . . Back to the Drama

Let's return to the place where we left off with Joseph, as all the puzzle pieces clicked into place. Just weeks before, Joseph had been a former Hebrew slave living as an Egyptian ruler. He spoke the Egyptian language, followed their customs, and filled their coffers, all the while retaining his true identity and fierce hope in a faithful God. Now his brothers kneeled before him, offering him their lives. He knew that his father was still alive and that his youngest brother was well. He knew that his brothers had not forgotten the details of the day when he was seventeen and they had sold him to nomadic traders. Even more, he saw the pain that choice still caused them—the ramifications of their guilt and the grief he knew his father carried. And when Judah offered his own life for Benjamin's, Joseph had seen everything he needed to see.

> *Joseph could no longer control himself before all his attendants, and he cried out, "Have everyone leave my presence!" So there was no one with Joseph when he made himself known to his brothers. And he wept so loudly that the Egyptians heard him, and Pharaoh's household heard about it.*
>
> *Joseph said to his brothers, "I am Joseph! Is my father still living?" But his brothers were not able to answer him, because they were terrified at his presence.*
>
> GENESIS 45:1-3

Joseph sent away his attendants—everyone who represented his new life. And in that moment, he became just Joseph again, the dreamer, the baby brother, the Hebrew, son of Jacob, brother of Benjamin. He was overcome as the uncertainty and confusion of the past two decades collided in his heart, and he began to weep. With joy? Healing? Sadness? All of the above? His weeping was so loud that everyone heard it. It was uncontrollable and came from deep within. It was vulnerable, cathartic, and courageous. Joseph no longer hid his identity or his pain. He was just Joseph.

But his brothers were terrified. When they last saw Joseph, he was a teenager, a young, impetuous boy. The person standing before them was a man, one with power, gravitas, wisdom, and strength. They could not reconcile the two, their vision perhaps obscured by the resentment and contempt with which they had originally viewed the young dreamer. Joseph walked closer to them, looked in their eyes, and with the very same skill that brought him from leadership in Potiphar's house and prison and now to Pharaoh's court, Joseph read their hearts. He told them: "Do not be distressed and do not be angry with yourselves for selling me here." He extended empathy and understanding, and then he sang his redemption song, the one he believed long before he met his brothers again: "It was to save lives that God sent me ahead of you" (Genesis 45:5).

God Did This

As Joseph revealed himself to his brothers, he consistently centered the story on what God was doing. He told them over and over, God did this. The work of redemption always takes us out of the center of the story. "God sent me ahead of you" (Genesis 45:5, 7). Joseph repeated it three times as he reassured his brothers (see also verse 8). Notice he did not dismiss the evil done to him; he did not call what was bad "good." He merely decentered himself in the story and allowed a good God to use the worst of circumstances. He called *that* good.

Redemption always centers on God and extends beyond ourselves. God holds together a bigger plan than the one we each live in. We are in a long, linked chain of relationships—those who have gone before us, those who will come after us. The choices we make today—to bless or to curse, to choose life or to choose death— eventually have ripple effects through our own family history.

Joseph believed that truth long before his brothers appeared before him. Joseph believed there was purpose in his pain long before that pain was relieved. Joseph lived his redemption song before knowing the end of the story. And when the ending finally came, Joseph's heart was full of gratitude and benevolence, not polite vengeance. Joseph was vindicated, but he didn't need to be vindicated to choose the redemptive song. Joseph was reconciled to his family, but he didn't need to be reconciled to them to believe that God had a plan. "It was to save lives," said Joseph. And the icing on the cake was that it had saved his brothers' lives too.

Here's the real power of redemption: God can free us even if full restoration never comes. Every season eventually changes. The grief lessens; we find glimmers of joy again. Life moves forward, and we embrace what's ahead. But we never forget where we've been, who we've been. We may still long for answers, for reconciliation, for forgiveness. But redemption is available despite what remains broken. It moves us from piercing pain to purposeful—and, yes, even beautiful—pain. It's the art God creates and the song we can sing.

> Redemption moves us from piercing pain to purposeful—and, yes, even beautiful—pain. It's the art God creates and the song we can sing.

In the moment of full vindication, Joseph wasn't worried about whether his brothers felt bad about what they'd done. They had suffered enough. Joseph met them with empathy. He wept over them. He kissed them. He asked about their father. That's the song of redemption. It propels us forward, and its fuel is always love.

The Long Arc of Redemption

My greatest difficulty in writing about redemption is not in believing that it was true for Joseph or in believing that it's true for you. It's in believing that it's true for me. Perhaps you can relate. Maybe the outcome of the season you're in is so uncertain and has been

NOT WHAT I SIGNED UP FOR

going on so long that you can't see a glimpse of redemption in the darkness. Perhaps you, like me, wonder if God is at work and if He might want to do something so great that your pain becomes purposeful. Some of us—probably more than you think—secretly doubt God's goodness in seasons like these, asking if we even want to worship a God who allows this much suffering in our world. My friend Justin says it this way:

> I tend to more readily "experience" God's redemptive intent in circumstances that are positive/pleasant/happy. In my mortal mind, when things turn out the way I want them to, when circumstances generate unexpected positive outcomes, it is easy to assume it is the result of His hand weaving redemptive thread into the tattered fabric of our lives. It usually hits me nearly instantly, in the moment.
>
> But when the hardships arrive, this is obviously much less the case.

When the hardships arrive, as they inevitably do, the only way to decenter our story is to widen the lens. Zooming out is about choosing to see this season in the midst of a whole life, a life impacted by the lives before it, around it, coming after it. We have to widen the lens enough that we see the shimmers of redemption in the dark corners, around the next bend. We have to dust for God's fingerprints in the past, to look back in order to look ahead.

I learned more about the long arc of redemption the day I pulled up to the concrete maze of a hospital parking garage, seven stories adjacent to another parking garage attached to the sprawling medical complex. As I navigated the path into the hospital, I passed a woman in a wheelchair at the curb, two nurses with stooped shoulders and tired eyes, and another woman crying into her phone. It had been eleven weeks since baby Mollie's birth to Stacie and JR, ten weeks since that horrible Sunday afternoon when Mollie's organs were shutting down and her medical team manually pushed oxygen into her lungs as she was transported to a trauma hospital. It had been seven weeks since she was awoken from a medically induced coma and removed from an artificial heart, three days since she'd had a seizure from medication withdrawals, and one day since she came off her last IV. Already her life had been a miracle fraught with more pain, more uncertainty, more twists and turns than any human believes they can bear—until they are in it.

When a crisis goes on this long, even the most faithful observers easily forget the toll it takes because life does have to go on. Stacie and JR had moved into temporary housing to be closer to the university hospital, but eventually JR had to go back to work. Each day, Stacie left her ebullient son, Gibson, with her mother or mother-in-law, who stayed with them in the apartment. Each morning she kissed her son goodbye (knowing that, on the bright side, her little boy was proof that God believes there is no such thing as too much joy), drove to the parking garage, rode up to the seventh floor, and walked into the windowless hospital room where she held her baby girl as she moved in and out of sedation. Every moment there, Stacie willed and prayed for Mollie's heart to strengthen and for her body to fend off the invisible germs that could make her sick. Stacie was riding out the storm of her life with patience and persistence.

On this visit, I stayed for an hour; Stacie had been there every day for months. We marveled together at baby Mollie's ability to beat the odds, stubbornly defying what the echocardiogram claimed her heart could handle, battling the virus that attacked her heart in the first place. But we were also sad, angry, and worried— sad about this happening in the first place, angry at what couldn't be fixed or changed, worried about what the future might hold.

Over mediocre sushi in the hospital cafeteria, we talked about redemption. "I think redemption has a long arc," Stacie said between bites of a tasteless California roll. She told me that before she and JR even started dating, each of them had watched young friends and family navigate difficult pregnancies and births. Both JR's sister and Stacie's friend ended up losing their babies. As a result, JR and Stacie—who were friends but dating other people at the time—had taken stock of their lives, reassessing what they would need in a spouse if they were to go through a time like that.

Soon after, the couple had connected, each with a fresh perspective on what they wanted in a partner. They knew they were looking for someone whom they could go through something like *that* with. The tragedy of losing a baby is never okay. We were not designed to nonchalantly accept that kind of grief and loss. But even in the terrible tragedies that JR and Stacie had witnessed, redemption shimmered. Back then, they dusted for prints and found God's hand at work in the lives of these bereaved parents. Little did they know they would find themselves in a similar place, or that they would discover strength and intimacy through this trial. Years later, both can look back at the time before they were even dating one another and marvel, "God knew this day would come. He prepared us by giving us one another."

Mollie was defying the odds and attesting to miracles as her little heart continued to heal. She spent several more weeks in the hospital, but little by little, her heart was getting stronger. Three months after that traumatic birth, she finally came home and met her big brother for the first time. As I write this six months later, she's eating, growing, smiling—making her way into the world with a redemption song we all want to sing about. There is still work ahead—and still healing to go for Stacie and JR.

Even when our story comes to a beautiful chapter, we have to process the pain and the trauma, because that's the real and redeemed way to live. It's an ongoing choice to sing our redemption song, even as we hold space for what is hard and painful and broken in life. The choice we make—the choice that brings life— is the decision to live the redeemed story in our own lives. This is the heart of the gospel of Jesus Christ. This is our living hope.

A PRAYER FOR WHEN YOU ARE SHORT ON HOPE

Father,

I find myself long on anxiety
and short on hope.
Sometimes . . . redemption just seems
too good to be true.

But maybe that's just it.

You are too good:
So good it's hard to believe You love me at my worst.

And You are too true:
So true that I have to relent and take You at
Your Word.

So here's the good truth:
It's all redeemable.
That it works together for good.
That it's part of a bigger story.
And You'll walk me through it.

And I think just that, God,
that's enough to hope for today.

Amen.

When they told him everything Joseph had said to them, and when he saw the carts Joseph had sent to carry him back, the spirit of their father Jacob revived.

GENESIS 45:27

CHAPTER 11

RESTORATION

*A revival is nothing else than
a new beginning of obedience to God.*

CHARLES FINNEY

As part of a military family whose parents had found God in the born-again evangelical movement of the 1980s, I attended services on military bases growing up. Other than occurring every Sunday, however, our worship experience differed from that of other churches in just about every way. I would loosely title our personal faith tradition "Patriotism, Piety, and the Protestant Chapel." On every military base where we lived, a chapel that functioned as a religious catchall was lodged somewhere between the commissary and the bowling alley. Catholic mass was held at 9 a.m.; Protestant church at 10:30 a.m. If we got there early enough or if the Catholic priest of the day got a little long-winded with his homily, we might arrive at the sanctuary in time to see the crucifix lowered from its exalted position behind the altar and the plain Protestant cross hefted up in its place. As a kid, I found this an odd experience: *Don't we worship the same God?*

Later, after my own seminary training in church history, I had a better sense of how we got to cross-swapping on Sunday mornings: Catholics assert that the crucifix places Christ's death in its proper role in our salvation; "We would not have the gift of salvation without Christ's crucifixion."[1] Protestants assert that the plain cross represents the hope of resurrection. After all, Jesus died on the cross but didn't stay there! (I can almost hear the pep rally–like worship song that would accompany this phrase at high school youth camps everywhere—and end up on a T-shirt.)

Maybe unexpected seasons are like that moment in between Sunday services in the military chapel when neither cross is exalted, when we live somewhere in between the painful reality of Christ's death and the promise of hope found in the empty cross. It strikes me that my faith tradition most certainly wanted to elevate the empty cross; to bring forth the hope of resurrection life, abundant life, free life. And those are good and beautiful things; but taken without the fullness of the story, they are also easily corruptible things. The Jesus dream comingles with the American dream; the cross is raised along with the flag, and we think that abundant living should feel like a pain-free life with 2.2 children and a house with a picket fence.

The empty-cross life often doesn't seem to have room for crucifix-cross suffering, so we assume that unexpected seasons must come because we've messed up, or we've been left behind, or we are being punished by a God who we've begun to believe brings victory only in the form of abundance, prosperity, and a comfortable life. This is the tangled, toxic roots of sin in our story, the very things that God unravels and uproots as we lose our identity and then refind ourselves in Him.

Unexpected seasons invite us to live in the mystery between the crucifix and the resurrection. As we walk forward in our uncertainty, or look back and ask God to redeem what's broken and painful, we need a way to frame our lives with room for both the cross where Jesus died and the empty cross where we are revived, restored, and refreshed. This gives us hope not just for the next life but for today—the today of dirty laundry, broken promises, unmet expectations, and ongoing tension. The hope for full redemption must be so present in our everyday reality that we *can* live with peace, courage, and joy, especially when we are surviving a season we didn't expect.

> Unexpected seasons invite us to live in the mystery between the crucifix and the resurrection.

This is the scene we find ourselves in as we go back in time to the end of Joseph's story, where we find him weeping and embracing his brothers, where sadness is being undone and life is being restored.

Redemption Is Real

In this final chapter of Joseph's redemption story, we see the promise of God's blessing coming full circle. Throughout this remarkable tale, we've seen God's covenant blessing continuing to move through His people. We've learned that God's blessings are not only about what is happening *to* you but what is happening *through* you.

Sometimes it's difficult to take the long view, particularly if you have experienced the ramifications of generational brokenness. Perhaps you have been forced to wrestle with your own healing because of sin that came before you. If you've encountered dysfunction in your family system, neighborhood, or church culture; if you carry scars or have been wounded by the wounds of those who came before, you understand the great and destructive power of sin. You know that sin has the power of death in it, not only for those who perpetrate it but also for those on the receiving end. You know that left unchecked, this brokenness will birth brokenness in your own story, so you often fear passing those same destructive patterns along to your own children.

And yet redemption is real.

Redemption is like a galvanizing force of positivity and heal-ing, spreading its way out from the source to everyone who comes in contact with it. The power and promise of the gospel is that although sin is powerful, grace is mighty.

That's the truth we see as we take a closer look at three char-acters who each sing their own redemption song as Joseph's story concludes: Judah, Jacob, and the brothers as a whole.

Judah: from passive to righteous

Judah is a secondary character in the story of Joseph, but he needs a closer look. Although we can't do justice to the fullness of his story, let's hit the highlights (if you can call them that):

- We met Judah when he was the brother who decided to sell Joseph. Although these motives seem better than those of the brothers who simply wanted to kill him, Judah participated as they threw Joseph in the cistern, sat down to a meal and listened as he pleaded for his life, and then conveniently sold him and pocketed some cash. Not exactly righteous.

- Genesis 38 is devoted to exposing the depths of Judah's passivity and shirking of responsibility in the years that fol-lowed. After tragedy struck his two older (and wicked) sons, he sent his daughter-in-law, Tamar, to live as a widow in her parent's house. In an "out of sight, out of mind" move, Judah tried to avoid taking care of her as the law of God required he should.

  Many years went by. Tamar ended up disguising herself and tricking Judah into sleeping with her so that she could have an heir who would provide for her safety and well-being. When Judah discovered that Tamar was pregnant, he recommended that she be burned to death for her sin. But Tamar turned the tables and revealed that it was actually

Judah who got her pregnant. (I know, I know, this is truly the stuff of reality dramas.) Judah hit bottom.

It was at the moment when Judah decided to confront reality that we see a glimmer of hope for his future. And from that rock bottom, he saw himself clearly: He exonerated Tamar, calling her "more righteous" than himself (verse 26). He did not take advantage of her again.

Judah was confronted with his own sin; and once he acknowledged it, we begin to see a turn in the story:

- After the brothers' first journey to Egypt, they were required by Joseph to return with Benjamin. Jacob refused, and Judah provided sacrificial leadership for his family by convincing Jacob to let his brothers return to Egypt with Benjamin. He guaranteed his brother's safety, pledging that his father should hold him personally responsible for Benjamin's well-being.

- Judah was the first to speak out on behalf of his brothers when confronted by Joseph on their second journey: "God has uncovered your servants' guilt. We are now my lord's slaves" (Genesis 44:16).

- After Joseph revealed himself and the brothers went home to tell Jacob the news, Jacob agreed that his family should join Joseph in Egypt. Judah was chosen to be the one who was sent ahead as an ambassador for the family (Genesis 46:28).

Judah's story is worth its own book, but in this quick review, we see how the very suffering and sin that placed Joseph in Egypt also became part of the redemption song for Judah. Through the confrontation with Tamar and his own reckoning with how he'd treated Joseph, Judah realized the ways he'd perpetuated injustice and then worked to rectify them.

God's redemption of Judah's story became obvious at the end

of his father's life, when Jacob gave a blessing to each of his sons. Actually, a better word for Jacob's proclamations over the twelve tribes of Israel might be *prophecies* because not every son's future was blessed. Reuben was told he would not excel, Simeon and Levi were cursed for their anger, and Dan was called a snake and Benjamin a ravenous wolf. Judah was no Boy Scout, as we've seen. Yet the blessing his father Jacob gave Judah is one of righteous leadership:

> *The scepter will not depart from Judah, nor the ruler's staff*
> *from between his feet, until he to whom it belongs shall come*
> *and the obedience of the nations shall be his.*
> GENESIS 49:10

Despite his failings, Judah lived into a redemption song. He was given the leadership role that was meant to go to the firstborn. And his tribe would be the very one from which the Messiah, Jesus, would eventually be born.

The story of Judah is one of persistence, the relentless nature of Judah's failings swallowed up by the even more tenacious love of God. Whenever you wonder if your actions have disqualified you from the blessings of God, remember Judah. He became a leader not despite the pain he inflicted on others but *because* of what that pain ended up doing in his own life. That pain woke him up to reality, and his response led to glimmers of redemption that continued down his generational line, shining its purest light in the person of Jesus, our great Redeemer!

Revival Is Promised

Redemption is a process, one that's ongoing and sometimes may feel unfinished. But revival is promised. Revival means many things in the church world, so let's start with the Latin roots of the word: "*re-* ('again') and *vivere* ('to live.')"[2] Revival is promised because Jesus is the giver of life eternal—we are promised that we will not just live but live *again*, fully healed, fully restored. Revival will come in its fullness in the new life of heaven, but it comes in little and big ways throughout our earthly life with Christ.

I listened to an interview recently with Kevin Thompson, a white evangelical pastor who felt pushed out of his church during the political and racial upheaval of 2020 and 2021. As he recounted his story, he talked about a key moment in his early twenties when, as a seminary student, some of the things he had believed and assumed growing up as a white evangelical Christian in the South were challenged:

> To my knowledge, seminary was the first time I ever
> had a Black professor. And here was this professor who
> probably had voted differently than my parents in every
> election ever. And yet, he loved Jesus.[3]

While in this class, one of Kevin's assignments was to preach a short sermon on Ezekiel 37, after which he would be critiqued by his peers. In this passage, God walks with the prophet Ezekiel, bringing him to an entire valley of death: a place of dead, dry bones. He then challenges the prophet: "Son of man, can these bones live?" (verse 3).

Kevin preached the message and received some warm comments from his peers, and then his professor spoke up. He asked whether Kevin realized that he had just spoken on one of the most famous passages in African American thought. But, his teacher continued, unlike Kevin, who had placed himself as the prophet as he preached this message, the Black church would always preach from the perspective of the dry bones. Kevin explained what his professor told him next:

> And finally, Dr. Smith says, Kevin, do you notice that
> every time you preach a passage, you're the person in

power? He said, have you ever considered that you need
to be rescued by Jesus? And it was just a really powerful
moment to show how I view everything in Scripture
as, I'm the powerful one that's doing wrong. I never
see myself as the one in desperate need on the side of
the road in the Samaritan's story. Or the thief on the
cross who needs saving. I never see myself in those
positions.[4]

The power of our unexpected seasons is that we can identify
with the dry bones, perhaps for the first time. Those dry bones
might be artifacts of a former life, one that is so broken and dead
that we can't imagine revival. Unexpected seasons may create an
identity crisis in our comfortable lives, but they give us a whole
new way to identify with the stories God tells. We can identify with
the loneliness of the imprisoned Joseph, the bitterness of Naomi,
the forsakenness of Hagar. We can identify with the laments of
David, the exhaustion of Elijah, the tears of Jeremiah. And we can
identify with the sufferings of Christ, who allowed His heart to
be broken open by the sufferings of this world, who allowed His
blood to be poured out for that very same world's redemption and
revival. His heart was broken open for your suffering. His blood
was poured out for your redemption.

Revival is about answering this question: *Son of man, can these
bones live?*

And live they do. God instructed Ezekiel to prophesy to the
bones, to tell the bones to hear the Word of the Lord. Of course,
God could have brought the bones to life Himself, could have just
shown Ezekiel His power—but instead, He invited Ezekiel to par-
ticipate in the process. "Prophesy to these bones!" He said (Ezekiel
37:4). The bones didn't immediately become living people again.
First they rattled together, then tendons held them together, and
then skin covered them. But even then, the story wasn't over. Now
God said to Ezekiel, "Prophesy to the breath" (verse 9). The bones

rattled, the tendons attached, the skin covered—but it was only after the breath entered them that "they came to life" (verse 10).

God repeatedly gives us stories—not of immediate revival but of the *process* of revival.

Jacob: from dejected to revived

We took a look at the story of Jacob, Joseph's father, in chapter 3. We know that Jacob wrestled with his identity and his desire for blessing for much of his life. And we know that losing Joseph was a life-wrecking experience for him. Jacob mourned his son for many days and then disappeared from the Joseph narrative. He appeared back on the scene decades later. When the brothers came back from Egypt to tell their father what had happened, we catch a glimpse into Jacob's summation of his lot in life: "Joseph is no more. . . . Everything is against me!" (Genesis 42:36). He went on to warn the brothers that if he lost his youngest son, Benjamin, as he lost Joseph, "You will bring my gray head down to the grave in sorrow" (verse 38). Jacob carried the pain from the loss of his beloved son like a shroud of death.

So you can imagine the shock and disbelief Jacob felt when his sons came back from their second journey to Egypt, claiming, "Joseph is still alive! In fact, he is ruler of all Egypt" (Genesis 45:26). When Jacob heard this and saw the Egyptian carts Joseph had sent back with them so they could load up their possessions, his "spirit . . . revived" (verse 27). After carrying all that death, after living out of grief and pain for so long, Jacob was so stunned that it was as if he came back alive. God breathed life back into an old, grieving man. The kind of life that came back to him is expressed here through the Hebrew word *hayah*, which means "to live anew, to refresh, to rebuild."[5] This same word is used in God's challenge of faith to the prophet Ezekiel when He asks about the potential revival of dry bones: "Son of man, can these bones live [*hayah*]?"

Can what's dry and dead live anew?

Can this life be refreshed? Can this be rebuilt?

Does God have the power to bring even the dead back to life? Does God have the power to bring what's dead in me to life?

The resounding answer to that question in the story of Joseph, in the story of Jesus, and in the story of you is *yes*. The redemption that came through Joseph transformed and revived Judah. It revived Jacob. And it advanced God's redemptive plan, a story that played out generation after generation with the redeeming hand of God working to bring blessing, grace, and favor to everyone who seeks Him with their whole heart (Deuteronomy 4:29). Jacob needed a dream, a night of wrestling, his brother's love, his son's return. The fulfillment of all his longings was a lifetime in the making—but revival did come.

In our unexpected seasons, no matter the struggle, we can hold on to this belief:

Redemption is real. Revival is promised. But it's always a process.

You can have hope. You can enter into this story with your desires and dreams. Give them to God and experience the good gifts He has in this season. Those gifts start with the *hayah* hope of revival and refreshment. But the *hayah* life isn't just about one miracle. It's the ongoing miracle of life breathed into your story, day after day, moment to moment. There may be times when you surge ahead and times when you sputter. There may be moments when you feel like you're drowning and others when you feel that you've learned to swim in the deep end. The promises of God aren't solely about the destination but about lessons along the way that we receive only when we desperately need God to be near, to guide us through our darkest times.

> The promises of God aren't solely about the destination but about lessons along the way that we receive only when we desperately need God to be near, to guide us through our darkest times.

One thing I love most about Jacob's story is where we find him at the end of his life. After all the twists and turns, the joy and grief, Jacob and his reunited family had settled in Egypt. The Bible tells us that seventeen years later, right before he died, Jacob's last act was worship. This is the very action that lands Jacob in the famous "hall of faith" chapter in Hebrews 11:

> *By faith Jacob, when he was dying, blessed each of Joseph's sons, and worshiped as he leaned on the top of his staff.*
> HEBREWS 11:21

Jacob isn't remembered for his deceit, his mistakes, or even his grief. He's remembered because of his faith, because of the long life of revival that meant when he was called home to heaven, he was found worshiping at the door.

Our Revival . . . It's a Process

The year of my fortieth birthday, I entered into a season of reflecting on where I'd been and where I was headed. Long before I began writing books, I had used writing as a way to process the deep end of life, the place where, it seems, I could connect the truth of God's Word with the truth of my soul. In one of my journal entries that year, I wrote, "I spent the first twenty years of my life learning how to hide and the next twenty years learning how to be found."

Life is a process, and the things we learn early are not unlearned easily. It takes time and trust—often after our unexpected seasons end—to begin processing where we've been. That might look like revisiting your story in a journal so that you can travel back to the past to "relearn" your own experiences through a redemptive lens.[6] It may look like processing with a friend or counselor or spiritual director, looking for the fingerprints of God on your story in a way that you weren't able (or willing) to see in the pain of the moment. Lori Gottlieb, therapist and author of *Maybe You Should Talk to Someone*, says: "We're all unreliable narrators of our own lives, but we can learn to edit the stories that keep us stuck."[7]

Once we understand that redemption is always a process, that grace and forgiveness and a new view on life are so profoundly impactful that they happen at the slow growth rate of a tree, we can be gentle with ourselves. Knowing that old habits die hard and change takes time, we can celebrate what has changed while being patient with what still feels stuck, broken, or tender.

Joseph's brothers: from anxious to at peace

Consider how this process of redemption and revival unfolded in the lives of Joseph's brothers:

- When Joseph first revealed himself to his brothers, he immediately told them not to "be distressed or angry with [themselves]" (Genesis 45:5, ESV). Earlier he had listened to them blaming one another for their troubles, which probably gave him a sense of how they were likely to respond once they knew who he was.

- Once Joseph had revealed his identity, the brothers inevitably would have remembered what they'd said in his presence before they recognized him: "Surely we are being punished because of our brother" (Genesis 42:21). The oldest, Reuben, added, "Now we must give an accounting for his blood" (verse 22). The story was so deep, the guilt so heavy that they immediately connected their present trouble to their past actions. Anyone who has lived with secret shame understands that those stories don't die quickly.

- As the brothers were leaving to bring their father and families back to Egypt, Joseph told them, "Don't quarrel on the way!" (Genesis 45:24). Some basic deduction would assume they were already arguing, which led to Joseph's admonition.

And then, after nearly two decades in Egypt with Joseph, Jacob died, and it became clear that the brothers' fears were still very much alive:

> *When Joseph's brothers saw that their father was dead, they said, "What if Joseph holds a grudge against us and pays us back for all the wrongs we did to him?" So they sent word to Joseph, saying, "Your father left these instructions before he died: 'This is what you are to say to Joseph: I ask you to forgive your brothers the sins and the wrongs they committed in treating you so badly.' Now please forgive the sins of the servants of the God of your father."*
>
> GENESIS 50:15-17

In his teenage years, Joseph had been envied and hated by his brothers for his favored status. And yet seventeen years after he'd forgiven his brothers and moved forward, they remained stuck in their stories and fear. The way of fear always leads to self-seeking, self-protecting choices. It's the smaller way to live. It's a life of scarcity and anxiety rather than abundance and freedom.

And so when his brothers came back to him, hiding behind their father's authority to protect themselves even after his death, what did Joseph do?

He wept.

He wept for the prison that they'd kept themselves in all of those years. He wept with grief and compassion over their persistent, unredeemed story, in which they seemed to think that the way they must atone for their sin was by being punished.

"We are your slaves," they told him, throwing themselves down in front of him (Genesis 50:18). The first time they bowed down in front of Joseph, they didn't know who he was. On this occasion, in perhaps the true fulfillment of Joseph's long-ago dream, they threw themselves down at his mercy, knowing who he was. Perhaps Joseph wept to discover that after all this time, they still didn't believe him. Perhaps he wept to know that they still thought he cared about them only because it would make Jacob happy. "We are your slaves" was a true statement in the deepest sense. They were still enslaved by their fear of retribution, their guilt, their past.

But redemption is always a process, and so seventeen years after first offering his brothers forgiveness, Joseph did so again. He did not get frustrated with them. He did not show resentment that they didn't believe him the first time. He simply offered grace again. He extended kindness, redirecting their lives into the redemptive story.

> *Joseph said to them, "Don't be afraid. Am I in the place of God? You intended to harm me, but God intended it for good to accomplish what is now being done, the saving of many lives."*
> GENESIS 50:19-20

Joseph invited them to move forward. He invited them to stop living in a story of death and curse and to choose the story of life and blessing. Old stories die hard. Our sin and shame enslave us.

And just as Joseph wept over the narrative that kept his brothers stuck, Jesus weeps over the broken things of the world—He weeps for those who grieve (John 11:35), and He weeps for those who are too prideful to accept the truth (Matthew 23:37). And out of His great compassion, Jesus invites us to choose the story of life over death, no matter how unexpected and difficult the circumstances might be. He extends grace to us not one time, but time and time again. If Joseph could extend this kindness to his brothers, imagine how much more Jesus extends His kindness to you.

If you've been enslaved by your sorrow or shame over what's happened in the past, throw yourself upon the mercy of Jesus, the One who can set you free. If you've been stuck in your story because of the bitterness of unforgiveness, throw yourself upon the mercy of Jesus, the One who can release you from this prison.

Redemption is a process that often takes a lifetime, a series of moments to reclaim what's been broken, wounded, or crushed by allowing God to make something new from all of it.

Jesus came to "reconcile to himself all things" (Colossians 1:20)—and that includes the way He's at work in your story. Some steps are done. Some remain undone. Some feel miles away from ever being repaired. But let the reassurances of Joseph to his brothers be the promises of God for you today:

Do not be afraid.
God is here.
God has plans to accomplish good for you and through you.

A PRAYER FOR WHEN YOU NEED TO MOVE FORWARD

My always-redeeming God,

*Help me to see the things You've already redeemed
in my life
as clearly as the things I always see still undone.
Give me the courage to keep extending grace,
forgiving me, forgiving others.
Help me accept the grace You have for me
right into the deepest part of myself
so that all that flows out of me
is that same loving-kindness.*

Amen.

Joseph is a fruitful vine,
    a fruitful vine near a spring,
    whose branches climb over a wall.
With bitterness archers attacked him;
    they shot at him with hostility.
But his bow remained steady,
    his strong arms stayed limber,
because of the hand of the Mighty One of Jacob,
    because of the Shepherd, the Rock of Israel.

GENESIS 49:22-24

CHAPTER 12

IDENTITY, REIMAGINED

Be like a bamboo. It bends, but
does not break; it's flexible, yet firmly rooted.

JAPANESE PROVERB

Living symbols of our stories are all around us. When I officiate a wedding, I particularly love the ring ceremony, the living symbol portion of the wedding. The couple repeat these vows to each other:

"This ring I give you, in token and pledge . . ."

"In token" gives the ring its meaning: *This ring serves as a symbol of what I want to convey.*

"In pledge" gives the ring its promise: *This ring serves as a promise of what I intend to commit.*

"This ring I give you, in token and pledge,
of my constant faith, and abiding love."

The unbroken circle of the metal band is a symbol of the promise, the hope, the future. The story of Joseph features robes of honor and a ring of identity. And our story is also one that includes robes and rings—the symbols God uses to describe our truest identity.

We all choose robes and rings to wear in life. We may have robes of status, rings of belonging. Our robes and rings are outward symbols of our inward reality, the roles we cherish: husband and wife, father and mother, daughter and son. We put on robes as judges and as clergy. We put on rings from our spouse, our schools, and our sports teams. We put on uniforms when we work in medicine or serve in the military. We put letters for our fraternity and sorority on our sweatshirts, and we put bumper stickers on our cars when our kids make the honor roll. We wear badges of honor that help us feel okay with our place in the world, that assure ourselves and others that we have a tribe, that we have status, that we belong.

But rings get lost. Promises get broken, and the symbols of our allegiance no longer fit because something outgrew us, or we outgrew it. Marriages fracture; love dissolves; the fire grows dim. Our hearts break over a million different things, whether in love, in life, in what was, or in what never will be.

But as true as those unexpected turns can be, redemption is still real, and revival is still promised. Circumstances change. Rings are found. Repentance is sought, and love can be born again. Life is a series of victories and losses, seasons of bewilderment and darkness followed by seasons of new hope again. But there is a promise that is never broken and an identity that never changes, even in our darkest times. That promise and identity exist in the truest part of us, a place that can never be touched by human hands or marred by human suffering.

Joseph, the Restored

In Joseph's story, robes are a key symbol that signify his identity and status. As a teen, Joseph was given a richly ornamented robe to signify his favored place in his father's eyes. Not long afterward, that very symbol of his favored life was stripped from him and given to his father as proof of his death. Stripped of robe, family, and tribe, Joseph traveled to Egypt without the symbols that had defined his identity.

He then wore the cloak indicating he was Potiphar's trusted steward, but he was stripped of that by Potiphar's wife during his test of integrity. He wore the clothes of a prison slave as he interpreted dreams for the baker and the cupbearer—and he wore this garb of humility for the longest chapter of all. And when Joseph was finally called to Pharaoh's presence and rightly interpreted his dream, "Pharaoh took his signet ring from his finger and put it on Joseph's finger. He dressed him in robes of fine linen" (Genesis 41:42).

These robes and ring indicated a new identity: He was now a governor of Egypt. As we know, true blessing always extends outward from the blessed, represented in this story by Joseph's new clothing. Then, after Joseph had revealed himself and reunited with his brothers, he gave each of them new clothing, signs of his power, honor, and provision (Genesis 45:22).

Identities were given, taken, stolen, returned. But through his faithfulness to God, Joseph revealed the much deeper identity he carried within, one that went even deeper than family and was stronger than success and more powerful than even the worst of his suffering. Joseph never forgot who God was and what God could do: "You intended to harm me, but God intended it for good" (Genesis 50:20).

Jesus, the Redeemer

In Jesus' story, robes also play a key role.

Scripture tells us that, over and over, Jesus put off in order to take up. Jesus put off His sandals at His baptism to begin His earthly ministry. He put off His outer garment to wash His disciples' feet. And in the greatest act of humility, He put off His perfect nature to take our sin upon Himself. Like the Passover lamb, He allowed Himself to be the sacrifice needed to atone for our sin.

The robe and ring are symbols of identity and belonging, so it's no wonder that Jesus used them in one of His best-known parables: The Prodigal Son found himself destitute, far from home and in rags because of his own waywardness. Yet when he came to his senses and returned home, his father rushed out to greet him, telling his servants, "Quick! Bring the best robe and put it on him. Put a ring on his finger and sandals on his feet" (Luke 15:22). Jesus said this is the kind of rejoicing that happens in heaven when a lost one returns home.

To be found by God is to first identify our true nakedness, our inability to clothe ourselves with external wrappings like success, relationships, or appearance—any of the outward coverings we use to try covering our inadequacies. To be found by God is to allow Him to be the One who covers us and gives us identity—to be dressed in the family robe, to be gifted the family ring. Robes and rings are symbols of our identity, our belonging, our tribe. And the robes and rings that God gives can never be taken away. Our robe of righteousness is a "garment of praise" (Isaiah 61:3), and our signet ring is a sign of our true identity, our status as children of God and coheirs with Christ.[1] Through His death and resurrection, we have become heirs with Christ, and to continue in His legacy is to "share in his sufferings in order that we may also share in his glory" (Romans 8:17). Suffering came to Christ in two ways: as a consequence of His enduring, boundless love for all people (not just the "good people") and His enduring, boundless obedience to God.

Unexpected seasons will ask us for both increasing love, even for our enemies, and increasing obedience, even when it hurts.

Unexpected seasons will also ask us for both: increasing love, even for our enemies; increasing obedience, even when it hurts.

As Jesus was nearing the end of His earthly ministry, when

He "knew that the Father had put all things under his power, and that he had come from God and was returning to God," He did a curious thing for one who has full knowledge of His power. He once again put down in order to take up: "[Jesus] got up from the meal, took off his outer clothing, and wrapped a towel around his waist" (John 13:3-4).

Unlike Joseph, who had been forcibly stripped of his robe, Jesus removed His willingly. In a foreshadowing of the offering He would make just a day later, He gave his disciples a living symbol of His sacrifice—laying aside His identity as the beloved Son so that we might have access to the Father through Him. And with His cloak laid aside, Jesus washed the disciples' feet. He told them, "I have set you an example that you should do as I have done for you" (John 13:15).

When Jesus went to the cross, He was again stripped of His clothing, but this time by rough hands. The Roman soldiers "put a scarlet robe on him, and then twisted together a crown of thorns" (Matthew 27:28-29). This robe became a symbol of mockery and violence. You can almost hear the demons cackle as they watched the Son of God being beaten, spit upon, flogged, and mocked by the very people He'd come to save. And yet this was the way—the way of redemption, the promise of revival.

Jesus was hung up on a cross, another symbol of shame. He put down His glory and allowed Himself to be lifted up for our good. In His greatest moment of sacrifice, we are given a view into great triumph: the persistent grace of God that's always extending to one more person. In the moments before Jesus' death, that one more was the thief on the cross next to Him, the one to whom Jesus said, "Today you will be with me in paradise" (Luke 23:43). To take up the identity of Jesus, to be clothed with His righteousness, always means we also take up the way of the Cross. We choose to be living sacrifices, allowing our pain to be transformed for God's glory, and His blessing to be conveyed through us for the good of others. We permit even what's stripped away to illuminate the identity that Jesus went to the cross to preserve—our identity as sons and daughters of God, whether we come to Him as dry bones or desperate criminals. There's always room for more.

Then from the cross with a loud cry, Jesus took His last breath, gave up His spirit, and declared the work finished.

Son of Man, can these bones live?

On that sad and sacred day, another man named Joseph stepped forward. He was a member of the Sanhedrin, the religious group that was so threatened by Jesus' claims. This Joseph, however, was different. Like our Joseph from Genesis, he faced a test of integrity: Would he have the courage to believe? When Jesus died, Joseph of Arimathea boldly asked Pilate for His body in order to prepare it properly for burial. He then removed Jesus' broken body from the cross and wrapped it in linen. In a way, this act served as a bookend to His birth, when the infant Jesus had been swaddled and placed in a manger. Then, too, He had laid aside His glory to come to us in the most vulnerable way possible.

After Joseph wrapped Jesus' body in linen, he laid Him in the tomb, the place of dry bones. Just a few days later, the disciples got word from the women who'd gone to anoint Jesus' body that the tomb was empty. Simon Peter, one of Jesus' disciples, ran to the tomb, which he entered, only to find the linen that had covered Jesus laid aside.

Son of Man, can these bones live?

Jesus' answer is a resounding *yes.*

Because of Christ, we are a family of redeemed and saved people. We serve a faithful and forgiving God, which gives us the strength to be faithful and forgiving sons and daughters. Joseph was wrongly treated and suffered in order to redeem his own family and eventually his people. But we serve a God who sent His own Son, who was wrongly treated and suffered unto death so that we might be redeemed as His people. Joseph was faithful to God in the thirteen years between his dream and its reality, between the prison and the palace—but Jesus is faithful throughout eternity, coming to earth as a faithful Son who "for the joy set before him . . . endured the cross, scorning its shame" (Hebrews 12:2).

We, the Redeemed

Joseph was able to make an entire family new. Jesus makes our eternal souls new. Joseph's family became the tribes of Israel, God's chosen people. Jesus' family becomes the new Israel, united as one under our eternal, loving Father who promises that when He comes again in glory, He will make everything new.

The way of the Cross was always the plan. Only a great love for a precious possession is worth great cost. And through Christ, God declared that we are His great love, His precious possession. This is the story that begins in Genesis and continues today: Our great and loving God extends His heart of mercy, love, and belonging, over and over again. Our great God covers our sin, redeems our past, and frees us to live out our future.

As humans, our story with God is one of continually messing up and God continually covering us with

Through Christ, God declared that we are His great love, His precious possession.

His love. All the way back to our origin story in Genesis, God has been covering us with His love and redeeming us for His glory. He covered us with clothing in the Garden of Eden after Adam and Eve first felt shame (Genesis 3). Later He promised us "a robe of his righteousness" as His chosen people (Isaiah 61:10). Because of our identity in Christ, we have the power to be clothed "with compassion, kindness, humility, gentleness, and patience" (Colossians 3:12).

The way God redeems our unexpected seasons will look different for each of us. Your season may change in an instant, or you may remain in it for life. But one day, all will be reconciled. All will be redeemed. No matter how it plays out, God wants you to trust Him and develop a resilient faith.

Such a faith is okay with pain—suffering alongside others without breaking under the weight. When you make the journey with Christ, your story will bear witness to the way that pain and suffering can actually be used to God's glory. Resilient faith knows that even though our Father in heaven almost never responds to our demands for explanations with clear answers, He has given us the one thing that cannot be disputed. He has expressed His good and powerful nature, not through an answer but through a life. That life is Jesus, who entered into our suffering, took on Himself the suffering we ourselves could never bear, and now offers us His comfort, presence, and glory in our suffering.

Joseph showed us a faithful life, an extraordinary life, a redeemed life. In his last recorded words to his brothers, he said, "God will surely come to your aid" (Genesis 50:24). From beginning to end, Joseph trusted a faithful God in a fickle world. The blessing his father left him before Jacob died speaks of Joseph's resilient faith. Because of God, his bow was steady. His arms were limber. His faith was resilient. His purposes were true. His was one story embedded in the great big story of God's redeeming love.

May your life speak only of the goodness of God, even in the trials. May you discover, in the putting down and taking up, in the gaining and in the losing, that you had nothing to fear. God was always there. And God used everything, even things intended for evil, for good.

A PRAYER OF RESILIENT FAITH

God of Abraham, Isaac, and Jacob,
God of Joseph and God of me,

Would You make me like the bamboo
that bends but doesn't break?
Would You show me today the bounty
  of Your goodness
in a trickle or a tidal wave?
Let me see the gifts You give:
Cover me with Your robe of righteousness,
array me in a garment of praise,
and clothe me with the things
that will bring You glory today.
Thanks for the way
You always cover for me.

Amen.

Conclusion

Perhaps like you, the pandemic gave my family time to take stock and consider moving to a new home. Our original plan had been to stay in our sleepy suburb until the kids graduated. Years before, we had settled into our comfortable house, which had space for our kids and their friends and was close to church and work. But in the disruption that followed the pandemic, we slowed our pace enough to recognize that the very reasons we had chosen to live in our neighborhood had all changed: We were between churches, work was now remote, and our kids had all chosen to attend a charter high school in the city. We felt excited about the idea of a new way of life, surrounded by more diversity and more closely aligned with what we sensed God was doing in our city. A year after the first conversation about a change, we sold our house at what we thought was surely the height of the market, moved into a rental in the city, and hoped our gamble would pay off.

We thought a rental home would be a great idea (spoiler alert: It was not). I struggled and prayed and kept healing and kept walking forward. The season felt long and lonely. It didn't feel like just a transition—somehow I began to believe that this pain was the new normal, that this foggy and uncertain season was the only thing ahead. But one ordinary morning as I sat with my Bible and journal, I wrote out my prayers, only to discover a deep lie I'd been carrying: *God, I don't think very highly of You.* It wasn't that I didn't serve God, worship God, or believe God. I just believed less of God because the season felt like less. I had stopped praying big dreams. I had stopped petitioning Him about the future. I had stopped praising Him for the past.

I carried that realization with me all that day, but by that evening, I decided to stop thinking less of God and brought Him my full, detailed petitions. I ended up with a seventeen-item checklist of what I was hoping for in a house, from details like "separate space for the kids to have friends over" to "natural light all times of the day." It wasn't a short list at all. But it was an important list because it was the moment when I trusted God again with my dreams. I felt the first breeze of revival moving into my heart in those bold and specific prayers. At one point I declared to the Lord: "I want to be living in the house you have for us so we can host Cameron and her friends getting ready for their prom."

On April 11, we put a contract on a house with fifteen of the seventeen items on my list (I see You, God). We moved in exactly thirty days later, on May 12, 2022. May 13, the very next day, was prom. Literally hours after we moved the couch into the living room and the pots into the kitchen, a half-dozen teenage girls filled our home with their curling irons and fake lashes and laughter, with the joy, lightness, and exuberance of youth. This is when I began to dream again, to believe that there would be a new season after a long and unexpected one that had caught me by surprise and lingered longer than I would have ever anticipated.

Fast-forward six months to the night of Halloween. Our youngest son invited his friends over and they walked the block over to Hanover Street, where the decked-out Halloween community tradition had been revived after pandemic restrictions. Thousands of people jammed the streets, filling up their buckets with candy until they overflowed. Our nephew Jack, fresh out of college and in his first grown-up job, showed up with his girlfriend, and they helped Dave and me set up appetizers and hand out candy.

Cameron showed up later with eight more friends—they were somewhere between teenagers and adults—and they listened to music around the firepit. Dave and I sat on the front porch, greeting every color, size, and stripe of family, from young couples with babies to friends with dogs, teenagers, and everyone in between.

A group of three teenage girls approached our porch, and one of them looked more closely at me. "You look familiar," she began, cocking her head slightly and tapping her Halloween nails to her face.

"Do you . . . go to church?" I asked.

It turned out they knew me from my previous ministry role, the one that I still missed but knew I had to leave. The mom in the background stepped forward. "Do you have a word for us? My daughter Chrissy has a surgery coming up. . . ." I stepped down from the porch, and Chrissy told me the story of her illness, her unexpected season. The worry she carried was etched across her face. And so right there in the middle of the crowds and the kids and the candy, I placed a hand on Chrissy's shoulder, and we formed a costumed huddle, praying for her healing, her connection to God's purposes for her, and her comfort.

Later that evening, a few twentysomethings I had previously mentored in a leadership program at our former church stopped by. We stood in a circle and laughed, and they told me how their tribe had multiplied through new marriages and friendships. I still worked with one of them, and we connected quickly about a few interviews we had the next day.

It turns out that sometimes it's only after you get lost for a while that you find out where you've always been, where you truly belong.

Sometimes it's only after you get lost for a while that you find out where you've always been, where you truly belong.

At the end of the night, Dave grinned at me. "All your dreams have come true."

It was not lost on me that on the day that we celebrate a

tradition of connecting with the dead, I had the chance to celebrate life, to worship the God of revival and redemption in the form of cheese dip, too much candy, laughter, prayer, and community. On the night of the dead, we celebrated life—real and redeemed life.

It's not a perfect or pain-free life. It's a life of triumph and tragedy. It's a life where redemption shimmers even though some things stay broken, some losses still sting, some questions are not yet answered. But it's my life, a life that I owe all to Jesus. And it's a life where God-sized dreams do come true, where I do not have to be afraid, where I can trust God to be God, and where even that which feels dark, broken, evil, or dead, God can use for good.

And you know what? I can sign up for that.

Acknowledgments

Books are like babies: All of them are special, but some have harder labors than others. This one required some extra special care. Here are a few of the faithful people I want to thank:

To my Tyndale team, Sarah, Jan, Kim, Kara, Jillian, and more: I had no idea when I first met Jan more than *a decade ago* (we are really getting old) that this would be not just a publishing team but a long-term, faithful partnership of love, advocacy, and ridiculous levels of support. Thanks especially to Sarah and Kim for this one: You both inspire me to be a better leader and a writer, and most importantly, a follower of Jesus.

To Jenni and the Illuminate Team: I feel like Goldilocks who finally found her perfect teammate. Jenni, you are that perfect fit: part sage, part strategist, part saint—I am so honored to be represented by you and to learn from the way you navigate the world of words for me.

To Gabe S., John and Lacy W., Erin R., Rachel T., Corey W., Aron G., Mike M., Scott M., and Don C.: You've carried me through in big and little ways that I am so grateful for. Thanks for being not just great pastors but great friends, and for sharing your own lives in a way that helps me have the courage to share mine.

To Stacie and JR: I can't write this without crying. Thank you for letting me walk with you through the valley of the shadow of death and see the love and grace of God overflowing to you both. When I wrote the dedication of this book, we truly did not know if Mollie would be with you by the end, and now she's the most beautiful, happy, healthy soul. I can hardly catch my breath when I think about the miracle, and I can't wait to celebrate all the beautiful, ordinary moments of life with your little fam.

To my almost-grown-up kids: Today I wrote in my journal "AH! I'm obsessed with my beautiful kids!" and I am. You guys are so loving and funny and inspiring, and you've loved us so well. Life isn't perfect, but it is beautiful. Dave and I will always be your biggest fans.

To Dave: You'll always be my best friend and the love of my life. Thanks for carrying my burdens when I'm weak, for sharing your wisdom when I get stuck, and for making me laugh when I want to cry. Oh, and for always doing the laundry and reminding me to be an adult when I forget. Couldn't be more blessed.

Notes

INTRODUCTION: LOSING THE HORIZON

1. *Joseph and the Amazing Technicolor Dreamcoat* premiered as a children's cantata in the late sixties before being developed into a full musical. This production was the first publicly performed collaboration by famed composer Andrew Lloyd Webber and lyricist Tim Rice, and the show made it to Broadway in 1982. See "Joseph and the Amazing Technicolor Dreamcoat," AndrewLloydWeber.com, accessed July 10, 2023, https://www.andrewlloydwebber.com/shows/joseph-amazing-technicolor-dreamcoat/.

CHAPTER 1: BELIEVE THE DREAM

1. These promises from Scripture are found in 1 Thessalonians 4:13-14; 2 Timothy 1:7; and John 15:11.

2. Eugene H. Peterson, *Eat This Book: A Conversation in the Art of Spiritual Reading* (Grand Rapids, MI: William B. Eerdmans Publishing Company, 2006), 44.

3. "Why We Can't Stop Bingeing Old Shows during the Pandemic," NPR, August 16, 2020, https://www.npr.org/2020/08/16/902977070/why-we-cant-stop-bingeing-old-shows-during-the-pandemic.

CHAPTER 2: HOLD ON TO THE PROMISES

1. Proverbs 1:7, AMP.

CHAPTER 3: THE TEST OF LOSS

1. A sermon given by Tim Keller entitled "Sent to Love," October 23, 2016, Redeemer Presbyterian Church, New York City; see also the *Gospel in Life* podcast, February 13, 2023, https://podcast.gospelinlife.com/e/sent-to-love/.

2. Sarah Epstein, "4 Types of Grief No One Told You About," *Psychology Today*, April 17, 2019, https://www.psychologytoday.com/us/blog /between-the-generations/201904/4-types-grief-no-one-told-you -about.

3. T. S. Eliot, "Part II: East Coker," *Four Quartets*.

4. This story can be found in Daniel 3.

5. See Genesis 16:13.

6. C. S. Lewis, *The Horse and His Boy* (New York: Collier Books, 1970), 158.

CHAPTER 4: THE TEST OF INTEGRITY

1. Vocabulary.com, s.v. "integrity," accessed March 1, 2023, https://www .vocabulary.com/dictionary/integrity.

2. "American Dream," Wikipedia, accessed May 6, 2023, https://en.wikipedia .org/wiki/American_Dream.

3. David Guzik, "Genesis 39—Joseph in Potiphar's House," Enduring Word, https://enduringword.com/bible-commentary/genesis-39/.

4. Guzik, "Genesis 39."

5. Mindi Thompson, "Patriarchs, Prostitutes and Potiphar's Wife: A Study of Genesis 38–39," *Leaven* 24, no. 4 (January 2016): article 10, https://digital commons.pepperdine.edu/cgi/viewcontent.cgi?article=2414&context =leaven.

CHAPTER 5: THE TEST OF HUMILITY

1. Proverbs 11:2, ESV.

2. Nipun Mehta, "The Radical Power of Humility," Daily Good, July 7, 2015, https://www.dailygood.org/story/1096/the-radical-power-of -humility/.

3. Jennifer Liu, "The US Moved Up in This Year's World Happiness Ranking—Here's Where It Ranks Now," CNBC Make It, March 19, 2022, https://www.cnbc.com/2022/03/19/world-happiness-ranking-2022-where -the-united-states-ranks-now.html.

4. Mehta, "The Radical Power of Humility."

5. Mother Teresa, *No Greater Love* (Novato, CA: New World Library, 2002), 55.

6. Luke 9:46-50.

7. Matthew 5:3-4.

8. Timothy Keller, *Jesus the King: Understanding the Life and Death of the Son of God* (New York: Penguin, 2016), 203–204.

9. I chose to quote this verse from the Amplified Bible because it conveys the absolute removal of Joseph from the cupbearer's mind, despite Joseph's care and help for him.

CHAPTER 6: TRUST HIM: KNOWING AND EXPERIENCING GOD

1. Jeffrey M. Jones, "Belief in God in U.S. Dips to 81%, a New Low," Gallup, June 17, 2022, https://news.gallup.com/poll/393737/belief-god-dips-new-low.aspx; Lindsey Witt-Swanson, Jennifer Benz, and Daniel A. Cox, "Faith after the Pandemic: How COVID-19 Changed American Religion," Survey Center on American Life, January 5, 2023, https://www.americansurveycenter.org/research/faith-after-the-pandemic-how-covid-19-changed-american-religion/.
2. Frank Newport, "Religion and Wellbeing in the US: Update," Gallup, February 4, 2022, https://news.gallup.com/opinion/polling-matters/389510/religion-wellbeing-update.aspx.
3. Jones, "Belief in God in US Dips," https://news.gallup.com/poll/393737/belief-god-dips-new-low.aspx.
4. Joshua 4:24.
5. *Forrest Gump*, directed by Robert Zemeckis, Paramount Pictures, 1994.
6. See 2 Corinthians 12:10 and 2 Corinthians 6:10. See also J. I. Packer, *Evangelism and the Sovereignty of God* (Downers Grove, IL: InterVarsity Press, 2012), 24–25.
7. See *Merriam-Webster Online Dictionary*, s.v. "antinomy," accessed May 22, 2023, https://www.merriam-webster.com/dictionary/antinomy.
8. Packer, *Evangelism and the Sovereignty of God*, 24.
9. Packer, *Evangelism and the Sovereignty of God*, 26, 29.
10. Packer, *Evangelism and the Sovereignty of God*, 24.
11. Packer, *Evangelism and the Sovereignty of God*, 40.

CHAPTER 7: TRUST THE OPPORTUNITY

1. J. Robert Clinton, *The Making of a Leader*, 2nd ed. (Colorado Springs, CO: NavPress, 2012), 117–118.
2. In the *Not What I Signed Up For Study Guide*, I provide journaling exercises to help you tell your story and discover your own *kairos* moments.
3. Samuel Emadi, *From Prisoner to Prince: The Joseph Story in Biblical Theology* (Downers Grove, IL: IVP Academic, 2022), 11.
4. You'll find examples of people praising God even through pain throughout Scripture, including Psalm 34:1-4; 69:29-31; Jeremiah 17:14; and Habakkuk 3:17-19.
5. See also Jeanne Stevens, *What's Here Now?: How to Stop Rehashing the Past and Rehearsing the Future—and Start Receiving the Present* (Grand Rapids, MI: Revell, 2022). Jeanne's book is a great resource for practicing the presence of God.

CHAPTER 8: TRUST THE TEARS

1. See Genesis 30:24.
2. Jerry Sittser, *A Grace Disguised: How the Soul Grows through Loss* (Grand Rapids, MI: Zondervan, 1995), 25.

3. Mandy Oaklander, "The Science of Crying," *Time*, March 16, 2016, https://time.com/4254089/science-crying/.
4. Richard Exley, *When You Lose Someone You Love*, (Colorado Springs, CO: David C. Cook, 2009), 21.
5. Henri J. M. Nouwen, Donald P. McNeill, and Douglas A. Morrison, *Compassion: A Reflection on the Christian Life* (New York: Image Books, 1982), 3–4.
6. Jesus prays in the garden of Gethsemane the night before His arrest and crucifixion, asking His Father, "If it is possible, may this cup be taken from me" (Matthew 26:39). You can also find the story in Mark 14 and Luke 22.
7. Henri J. M. Nouwen, *The Inner Voice of Love: A Journey Through Anguish to Freedom* (New York: Doubleday, 1996), xvi.

CHAPTER 9: GLIMMERS OF REDEMPTION

1. *Hebrew-Greek Key Word Study Bible* (1996), s.v. "*metanoeō.*"
2. For help navigating this area, check out *The Miracle Moment* (Carol Stream, IL: Tyndale, 2021). I wrote this relationship repair manual to offer help with engaging in healthy conflict and working toward reconciliation. Although Christ calls us to be loving, He also calls us to be shrewd.
3. C. S. Lewis, *The Great Divorce* (New York: HarperOne, 2001), 75. Italics in the original.
4. Martin Luther, "A Sermon on the Three Kinds of Good Life for the Instruction of Consciences," William R. Russell and Timothy F. Lull, eds., *Martin Luther's Basic Theological Writings*, 3rd ed. (Minneapolis: Fortress, 2012), 136.
5. Oswald Chambers, *My Utmost for His Highest*, "Decreasing into His Purpose," March 24, (Uhrichsville, OH: Barbour, 1935, 1963, 2014).

CHAPTER 10: REDEMPTION: THE LONG STORY

1. Ian McCann, "'Redemption Song': The Story behind Bob Marley's Timeless Anthem," uDiscover Music, February 6, 2023, https://www.udiscovermusic.com/stories/bob-marley-redemption-song-story/.
2. Richard M. Lerner, Michael E. Lamb, and Alexandra M. Freund, eds., *The Handbook of Life-Span Development: Social and Emotional Development*, vol. 2 (Hoboken, NJ: Wiley, 2010), 196. Studies include Erikson, 1963; McAdams, 2006; McAdams, Diamond, de St. Aubin, & Mansfield, 1997; McAdams et al., 2001.
3. Dan P. McAdams, "The Psychological Self as Actor, Agent, and Author," *Perspectives on Psychological Science* 8, issue 3 (May 2013): 272–295. This quote appears on page 288.
4. *Merriam-Webster Online Dictionary*, s.v., "redeem," accessed May 4, 2023, https://www.merriam-webster.com/dictionary/redeem, emphases mine.

5. After hearing her story, I fact-checked this and was delighted to discover it's true: "Fire burns off woody debris and exposes the soil, it creates an ash layer that returns nutrients to the soil and increases sunlight by killing some of the competing pines and firs." See "Giant Sequoia and Fire: The Past, Present, and Future of an Ancient Forest," Save the Redwoods League, accessed July 14, 2023, https://www.savetheredwoods.org /interactive/giant-sequoia-and-fire/.

CHAPTER 11: RESTORATION

1. "Embrace the Crucifix Instead of a Plain Cross? What's a Catholic to Do?" *Daily Bread*, The Catholic Faith Store, https://www.catholicfaithstore.com /daily-bread/embrace-crucifix-instead-plain-cross-whats-catholic/.
2. *Online Etymology Dictionary*, s.v. "revive (v.)," accessed May 4, 2023, https://www.etymonline.com/word/revival.
3. "The Pastors Being Driven Out by Trumpism," *The Daily* podcast, September 23, 2022, https://www.nytimes.com/2022/09/23/podcasts /the-daily/evangelicals-trumpism.html.
4. "The Pastors Being Driven Out by Trumpism," *The Daily* podcast.
5. *Hebrew-Greek Key Word Study Bible* (1996), s.v. "*hayah*."
6. If you need help processing your story, you might check out my book *The Struggle Is Real*, which provides a framework for understanding your old story and embracing a redemptive, hopeful version.
7. Lori Gottlieb (@LoriGottlieb1), Twitter, January 26, 2020, https://twitter .com/LoriGottlieb1/status/1221499146244198400.

CHAPTER 12: IDENTITY, REIMAGINED

1. Centuries after Pharaoh placed a signet ring on Joseph's finger, the prophets sometimes referred to Judah's leaders as God's signet ring, a sign of the Lord's rule over His people (Jeremiah 22:24; Haggai 2:23).

About the Author

Nicole Unice is a pastor and leadership coach who facilitates environments of safety and vulnerability so that leaders and teams can courageously identify obstacles keeping them from their maximum potential. As a sought-after speaker, Nicole has a down-to-earth style that allows even the largest gathering to feel conversational. Nicole is the author of several books focused on spiritual transformation and is a featured speaker through RightNow Media and Punchline. She holds degrees from the College of William and Mary and from Gordon-Conwell Theological Seminary. Nicole and her husband, Dave, live in Richmond, Virginia, with their three children and two pups. Visit her online at nicoleunice.com.

rightnow MEDIA

FREE BIBLE STUDY VIDEOS FOR

NOT WHAT I SIGNED UP FOR

Because you have purchased *Not What I Signed Up For*, you also have free access to the companion Bible study videos—perfect for group study or personal devotions.

Scan this code to access these videos for free!

Have you ever found yourself in an unexpected season, thinking (and saying to God), *This is not what I signed up for*? Join popular Bible teacher Nicole Unice, who helps you see how God uses life's hard times, twists, turns, and in-between spaces to grow something essential in your soul.

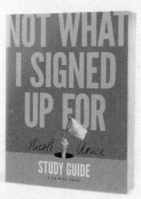

Not What I Signed Up For:
This book provides accessible tools to help you navigate the unexpected and disorienting seasons of life with strength, hope, and perspective. Drawing from the biblical story of Joseph, Nicole demonstrates how you can move through trial and temptation to trust.

*Not What I Signed Up For Study Guide:
This is a six-session workbook companion to the *Not What I Signed Up For* book. It's a great resource for church groups, Bible studies, and anyone who desires to navigate life's unexpected and chaotic seasons in order to find renewed hope and purpose.

It's time to transform your relationships at home, in love, and at work.
Are you ready for your miracle moment?

The Miracle Moment Discover the moment in every conversation that can change the whole relationship. Popular speaker Nicole Unice helps you discover the practical tools, words, and boundaries that will transform conflict into connection—even when you're tempted to shut up, blow up, or give up.

The Miracle Moment Participant's Guide A six-session workbook created for group or individual use. Accompanying DVD available for purchase. Streaming videos provided online at rightnowmedia.org.

Visit Nicole online at nicoleunice.com.

CP1686